Driving Digital Transformation

BUSINESS STRATEGIES

FOR ENTREPRENEURIAL VENTURES

Driving Digital Transformation

BUSINESS STRATEGIES

FOR ENTREPRENEURIAL VENTURES

FALIH M. ALSAATY

ARPress
ILLUMINATING IDEAS
EMPOWERING VOICES

ARPress
45 Dan Road Suite 5
Canton MA 02021
Hotline: 1(888) 821-0229
Fax: 1(508) 545-7580

Ordering Information:
Quantity sales. Special discounts are available on quantity purchases by corporations, associations, and others. For details, contact the publisher at the address above.

Printed in the United States of America.

  ISBN-13:   Paperback   979-8-89356-241-5

Library of Congress Control Number: 2024912189

Table of Contents

Chapter 1
The Emergence of AI-Driven Entrepreneurs in the Era of Digital Transformation

Chapter 2
Introduction to Business Strategies

Chapter 3
Guidelines to Business Strategies Formulation

Chapter 4
The External Environment and Strategy Development

Chapter 5
Types of Business Strategies

Chapter 6
Executing the Strategic Plan

Chapter 7
Digital Entrepreneurship

Chapter 8
Innovation and Artificial Intelligence (AI)

Chapter 9
The Entrepreneurial Mindset

Chapter 10
Digital Marketing

Chapter 11
Self-Leadership

Preface

This book is a practical guide for entrepreneurs aiming to grow their digital or traditional businesses. It offers strategies, real-world examples, and actionable advice to propel your venture forward. Written in accessible language, it's suitable for anyone, regardless of prior business knowledge.

The book provides comprehensive insights for beginners and seasoned professionals, helping you achieve your objectives and develop successful business strategies. It covers essential entrepreneurial concepts, such as launching new enterprises and seizing opportunities. It highlights creative, strategic entrepreneurs who turn ideas into value, maintaining competitiveness and profitability.

Championing entrepreneurial excellence, the book features visionary leaders who push technological and economic boundaries. It aims to inspire and guide your entrepreneurial journey toward growth and success with strategies for leveraging AI, digital technologies, and an entrepreneurial mindset to maximize your impact and contribute positively to society.

Designed to be easily understood, the content is valuable for anyone looking to advance their business or deepen their understanding of digital entrepreneurship, digital marketing, and strategic planning. Regardless of your experience level, this book supports your journey toward mastering digital entrepreneurship and building a robust, sustainable enterprise.

Key takeaways include:

- Learning effective strategies like differentiation, diversification, and integration.

- Embracing innovation and the desire to effect positive change.

- Utilizing digital platforms and software to launch and strengthen businesses.

- Developing an entrepreneurial mindset, crucial for success across industries, characterized by relentless opportunity-seeking and resilience.

Dedication

This book celebrates entrepreneurs who drive progress through bold vision and innovative solutions to create value, employment, and economic prosperity.

.

About the Author

Dr. Alsaaty is a Professor of Management in the Management, Marketing, and Public Administration Department at the College of Business, Bowie State University, Maryland. He received his MBA and PhD degrees from the Graduate School of Business Administration (Stern School of Business), New York University, New York. Dr. Alsaaty has extensive teaching and research experience in Management, Business Strategy, and Entrepreneurship. He taught at several universities in the United States and abroad. Dr. Alsaaty has numerous publications in professional journals. In addition, he has authored and co-authored the following books in recent years:

- Entrepreneurial Edge – Essential Skills for Business Success (2023).

- Entrepreneurial Reach (2012).

- Launching and Managing New Ventures (2007).

PART 1

UNDERSTANDING BUSINESS STRATEGIES

Chapter 1

The Emergence of AI-Driven Entrepreneurs in the Era of Digital Transformation

"All our dreams can come true, if we have the courage to pursue them."

Walt Disney

Chapter Objectives

- Gain an understanding of AI-driven entrepreneurship and its importance.

- Delve into the various facets and dimensions of entrepreneurship.

- Comprehend the prerequisites for securing venture financing.

- Grasp the fundamental concepts of digital transformation.

Entrepreneurship is a captivating and enthralling field that has been revolutionized by numerous entrepreneurs worldwide. These visionary individuals are crucial in creating value, seeking opportunities, and driving innovation across various industries and sectors. The recent release of the CNBC 50 Disruptor Companies[1] Showcases the quick rise of entrepreneurial ventures focused on disruptive innovation, especially in the United States. These ventures leverage cutting-edge technologies like artificial intelligence (AI), generative AI (GAI), robotics, quantum computing, and the metaverse. Entrepreneurs with a long-term strategic

---

[1] See, for example, the 2024 CNBC 50 disruptor companies.

vision utilize these technologies to develop and market high-quality products and services at competitive prices.

Entrepreneurs employing disruptive innovation strategies often introduce cost-effective products to address unmet consumer needs or create new ones. This approach often leads to creating new markets domestically and internationally, with superior business models and effective marketing tactics. Without robust business and functional strategies, companies risk becoming obsolete. Therefore, well-executed strategies are crucial for entrepreneurial success, driving sustainable growth and competitiveness.

What is Entrepreneurship?

After examining numerous dictionaries and textbooks' definitions[2], it becomes evident that entrepreneurship entails the journey of recognizing and pursuing opportunities to establish, oversee, grow, and sustain a venture[3] with the primary objective of attaining financial prosperity or positively impacting society. It necessitates a readiness to confront financial and other uncertainties throughout the endeavor.

Entrepreneurship is an ongoing journey comprising a series of interconnected actions that commence with establishing a venture and persist until its culmination. The primary objective of venturing into business is to attain a competitive advantage in the market and achieve a reasonable return on investment by creating value for customers by providing uniquely designed products or services.

This process involves identifying and anticipating financial, legal, and other risks by the entrepreneur and the entrepreneurial team. It necessitates a deep understanding of the product, technology, industry, economic sector, target market, and customer needs and desires.

---

[2] For example, Oxford Dictionary defines entrepreneurship as "the activity of making money by starting or running businesses, espe-cially when this involves taking a financial risk; the ability to do this", while Heidi, N. M. et al. (2018, p.6) define it as "discipline that seeks to understand how opportunities are discovered, created, and exploited by whom, and what consequences", *Entrepreneurship*, Los Angele: California, Sage Publishing.
[3] In the book, the terms venture, business venture, firm, company, corporation, enterprise, and business enterprise are used inter-changeably.

To establish a sustainable and profitable venture, visionary leadership, innovation, the strategic utilization of appropriate artificial intelligence (AI) technology, effective teamwork, a dedicated workforce, a perpetual quest for opportunities, and strategic planning are essential. Furthermore, a well-developed and well-structured business plan is indispensable. It guides leadership actions and activities while attracting investors during the venture's startup and growth phases.

A growth-oriented entrepreneurial mindset propels successful entrepreneurs. They emphasize market research and continuously expand their professional and social networks. They possess self-leadership qualities and exhibit adaptability to change circumstances and customer demands, enabling them to thrive in dynamic environments.

Who is an Entrepreneur?

Do entrepreneurs stand apart from the rest of society? Are they shaped by their upbringing or inherently born with entrepreneurial qualities? The perspectives of scholars vary on this matter. Some argue that external factors like education, experience, and networking shape entrepreneurs, while others believe they possess inherent traits that make them influential leaders in business and industry. As entrepreneurship programs and training have rapidly proliferated, particularly in the United States, and the number of entrepreneurs has grown exponentially, it seems more likely that entrepreneurs are molded rather than naturally gifted with their abilities.

According to the Oxford Languages Dictionary, an entrepreneur is "a person who organizes and operates a business or businesses, taking on greater than normal financial risks to do so". Entrepreneurs have a strong business orientation, are self-motivated, and tend to establish innovative ventures that introduce fresh business concepts, reshape existing ones, or revitalize outdated ideas - all while recognizing the potential risks involved. Accomplished entrepreneurs can identify, evaluate, and seize new opportunities, leveraging them intelligently to generate profits and foster prosperity.

What makes a person a successful entrepreneur? While a simplistic and potentially misleading response suggests that anyone with a bit of imagination and a moderate appetite for risk can achieve entrepreneurial success, this notion is not entirely accurate. Building a viable business enterprise requires more than just imagination and a willingness to take risks.

As stated by de Bono[4], A creative idea is one path to success... as is the ability to strike deals. So is the formation of a purposeful team. In reality, establishing a thriving venture necessitates a combination of various elements. These include possessing an entrepreneurial mindset and leadership skills, securing adequate funding, comprehending the market, demonstrating persistence, engaging in careful strategic planning, and responding to consumer demands for products or services.

It is important to note that although not everyone can establish a thriving and sustainable business, it does not diminish the importance of other career opportunities or personal achievements. Every individual has distinct attributes and strengths, and engaging in activities that resonate with those qualities in alternative domains is crucial.

Growth of Entrepreneurial Ventures[5]

Over the past forty years, there has been a significant increase in the number of entrepreneurial firms in the United States, as evidenced by available data. From 1980 to 2021, the number of firms that employ less than 20 individuals grew from 3.3 million to 5.7 million, marking a substantial growth rate of approximately 71 percent (Table 1). This expansion in entrepreneurial ventures also translated into increased employment opportunities on a national scale.

In 1980, these firms employed 16.3 million individuals, which rose to 21.7 million by 2021, indicating a 33 percent increase. Notably, these entrepreneurial firms employed 16.5 percent of the private sector's total labor force of about 133 million in the country in 2021.

To provide a visual representation of this data, Table 1 has been included as an invitation to aspiring entrepreneurs, encouraging them to prepare

---

[4] de Bono, Edward (1978). *Opportunities*, New York: NY, Penguin Books, Inc.
[5] While it is important to note that the U.S. government does not distinguish between entrepreneurial and non-entrepreneurial firms, this book considers entrepreneurial firms to encompass all enterprises with fewer than 20 employees.

for establishing innovative and growth-oriented business ventures.

Table 1
Entrepreneurial Firms in the United States
(Employment of less than 20 Individuals, 1980-2021)

Year	Number of firms	Firms' employment
1980	3,316,331	16,256,419
1990	3,922,757	20,196,312
2000	4,310,037	21,971,042
2010	4,427,405	20,936,643
2020	4,659,877	21,930,709
2021	5,667,878	21, 663,660

Source: U.S. Census Bureau, www.census.gov.

The rise in entrepreneurial firms in the United States and their ability to create more employment opportunities can be attributed to various factors. These include the political stability of the country, as well as the population's inclination towards entrepreneurship. The government's support for entrepreneurial endeavors through legislation, grants, and loan guarantees has also played a significant role.

The availability of accessible funding for entrepreneurial ventures, facilitated by venture capitalists, angel investors, individuals, and financial institutions, has contributed to this trend.

Furthermore, a favorable investment environment has further fueled the growth of entrepreneurial firms in the country.

AI and Digital Entrepreneurs

When exploring the realm of entrepreneurship, authors often distinguish between AI entrepreneurs and digital entrepreneurs. This differentiation is based on the belief that AI entrepreneurship primarily revolves around AI technologies and their applications in generating goods and services. It also includes AI-driven solutions involving machine learning algorithms and natural language processing systems. AI technologies encompass various areas like cybersecurity, fraud detection, and predictive analytics, which serve as focal points for AI entrepreneurs.

On the other hand, digital entrepreneurs utilize a wide array of digital technologies, including AI, to create innovative products and services. Their focus areas may encompass digital arts, e-commerce, and online business courses. However, in this book, we refrain from drawing a distinction between AI entrepreneurs and digital entrepreneurs for the following reasons:

1. The differentiation between AI entrepreneurs and digital entrepreneurs lacks justification and appears arbitrary.

2. The fields of AI technologies and digital technologies are intricately intertwined, with overlapping areas of expertise and opportunities for collaboration.

3. The landscape of AI and other technologies is rapidly evolving and diverse, particularly due to the accelerated pace of invention and innovation in recent years.

4. It is entirely conceivable that AI entrepreneurs, through diversification or integration strategies, expand their business scope to encompass digital products and services. Similarly, digital entrepreneurs may broaden their ventures to incorporate AI as a core component of their goods and services.

Considering these factors, we acknowledge the interconnected nature of AI and digital entrepreneurship, recognizing the potential for convergence and collaboration between these two domains.

Who is an AI Entrepreneur?

An AI entrepreneur is an individual who actively seeks a specific business venture involving using artificial intelligence and related technologies to perform tasks that typically require human intelligence. Like other entrepreneurs, the AI entrepreneur assumes an above-average amount of risk associated with the venture but also stands to benefit the most if the venture succeeds. They are expected to possess knowledge of the emerging and diverse technologies that enable AI applications, such as predictive analytics, natural language processing, and machine learning. Additionally, an AI entrepreneur is willing to experiment with new methods of creating value for customers and society through AI. They strive to introduce innovative products and services that leverage AI to solve problems, enhance experiences, or create new opportunities. Furthermore, an AI entrepreneur possesses a growth mindset and remains open to learning from data, feedback, and failures.

According to the definition, an AI entrepreneur is an individual who combines their entrepreneurial spirit with a deep understanding and utilization of emerging and diverse technologies. They possess a unique blend of skills, including a risk-taking attitude, a relentless pursuit of innovation, and a growth mindset. An AI entrepreneur thrives on exploring cutting-edge technologies such as generative AI.

They actively seek opportunities to leverage these technologies to create transformative and disruptive products and services. Risk-taking is a core characteristic of an AI entrepreneur. They understand that innovation often involves uncertainty and are willing to take calculated risks to push boundaries and challenge the market's status quo and business models. They embrace failure as a learning opportunity.

Introducing innovative products and services is a hallmark of an AI entrepreneur. Like other creative entrepreneurs, they are keen to identify market gaps and unmet needs. They have a knack for envisioning possibilities and combining AI capabilities with entrepreneurial insights to develop pioneering offerings. A growth mindset is an essential trait of an AI entrepreneur. They embrace learning and personal development, recognizing that the field of AI is ever-evolving.

To sum up, an AI entrepreneur is an ambitious, forward-thinking individual who harnesses the power of emerging technologies, takes risks, introduces innovative products and services, and embraces a growth mindset. AI entrepreneurs play a crucial role in driving the advancement of AI and its applications, shaping the future of industries and economic sectors worldwide.

Venture Creation

As previously mentioned, the data in Table 1 clearly shows that millions of individuals have started their own businesses in the United States in recent years. While some have become highly successful entrepreneurs, others have faced challenges and have not been as fortunate. This leads us to the question: what drives people to embark on their entrepreneurial journeys despite the uncertainties, risks, and potential for failure?

The following are the key factors that motivate individuals to pursue entrepreneurship in general, and specifically engage in AI entrepreneurial activities:

- The advent of AI technologies has opened up many opportunities for creative entrepreneurs to establish business ventures across various economic sectors and industries.

- The availability of funding to support viable startup ventures that offer unique products or services.

- Access to talented professionals and other valuable resources in different fields, making it easier for entrepreneurial teams to come together.

- The aspirations of well-educated and experienced individuals who seek wealth, fame, leadership, and influence by venturing into entrepreneurship.

- There are vast prospects for the AI market in the coming years, with significant opportunities awaiting. For instance, it is projected that by 2030, the AI industry will surpass $1.8 trillion in value.[6]

- The motivation of individuals to capitalize on perceived market opportunities.

- Government backing for establishing new ventures, particularly in the United States.

- A favorable investment environment within the country.

- The widespread availability of entrepreneurship programs in colleges and universities that encourage students to pursue careers in entrepreneurship.

- Influence from family members, friends, or social networks.

---

[6] Parmanandani, Niha (April 25, 2023). 10 Top Profitable AI Business Ideas to Lunch in 2023, OpenXcell, www.openxcell.com

- Limited availability of suitable employment opportunities.

Entrepreneurial Ventures and AI: Benefits and Implications

AI has brought significant advantages for entrepreneurial ventures, transforming how they function. One of the most notable benefits of AI is its ability to make superior decisions based on vast data sets. AI can analyze large amounts of data in real time, enabling entrepreneurs to make swift and effective decisions that improve business outcomes. Data driven decisions have more impact than those based on personal intuition. Data analysis is increasingly used to identify trends, patterns, and environmental risks.

Another significant benefit of AI is task automation, which enhances productivity and performance. By automating routine tasks, entrepreneurs can save time and scarce resources to focus on more critical activities such as market analysis, strategic planning, and innovation. Automation can also lead to more efficient and profitable operations.

AI also enables the adoption of innovative business models, making it easier to interact with customers. For example, chatbots can engage customers and provide them with product information and recommendations.

Personalization of goods and services is another benefit of AI. Recent research suggests that AI algorithms can analyze customer behavior and preferences, allowing enterprises to offer personalized product recommendations. This can increase customer satisfaction, loyalty, and business growth.

AI has the potential to revolutionize how businesses operate by providing insights from large data sets, automation, and innovative business models. The benefits of AI outweigh the potential drawbacks, such as the elimination of low-skilled jobs and the disappearance of many inefficient small firms. Entrepreneurs who embrace AI can gain a significant competitive edge and position their ventures for success in a highly competitive business environment.

AI technologies and applications offer power, flexibility, and diversity that can help companies grow and thrive. Companies can leverage AI to achieve their growth-oriented goals by adopting strategies such as differentiation and diversification.

Entrepreneurs should develop business strategies incorporating appropriate software and leverage AI and human skills to capitalize on these benefits fully.

Attributes of Entrepreneurial Companies[7]

Entrepreneurial companies in the United States have gradually shifted their business models, emphasizing deploying AI-related technology and highly talented workforces. The business models of these newly established ventures align more closely with changing market sentiment, consumer demand, and the evolving landscape of international business activities. The main attributes include the following:

- Emphasis on utilizing advanced technologies, including generative AI tools.

- The founders' vision focuses on introducing new or improved products and services.

- Organizational structure in many of these ventures is lean, flat, and designed to achieve efficient team effectiveness.

- They strive to accomplish more with fewer resources, such as capital.

- They actively seek out new customers and explore untapped markets.

- Strategic decision-making is centralized in the hands of the entrepreneur or the entrepreneurial partners.

- Many of these companies have a global orientation, with their geographic horizons extending beyond specific localities, states, or countries.

---

[7] See, for example, Gourevitch, Antoine (May 17, 2021). Meeting the Challenge of Deep Tech Investing, Boston Consulting Group, https://www.bcg.com/publications/2021/overcoming-challenges-investing-in-digital-technology

Business Models

Companies' crucial decision is how to effectively deliver their products and services to consumers or end users. This choice has a significant impact on the company's business model, which can be defined as the overarching plan to generate profit by selling a product or service, according to Maryville University.[8] The business model outlines the company's plans for production, service provision, and marketing, while also considering the associated expenses. Different business models exist to cater to various types of companies and industries.

Essentially, the business model determines the company's profitability by comparing its total revenue to its total costs over a specific period, such as a year. It reflects how the company conducts its business activities through physical stores (brick-and-mortar), online platforms, or a combination of both (hybrid model).

When examining the historical perspective, brick-and-mortar represents one of the earliest forms of business models. Another ancient business model involved the personal delivery of products, such as goods, stones, or animals, which were sold or exchanged through barter transactions.

Business models are not rigid structures within a business enterprise. They have the capacity to evolve, be discarded, altered, or integrated with other newly embraced models as the enterprise expands. The fundamental objective of business models is to streamline the enterprise's selling activities to enhance its profitability.

To maximize their operational potential, businesses that rely on AI technologies or offer AI-related products and services, like cloud computing providers, have recognized the need to innovate new business models or adapt existing ones. This allows them to improve revenue generation and effectively market their offerings.

Various authors have discussed different types of business models applicable to high-technology startup ventures and other businesses. For instance, Wiener et al. (2020)[9] have identified three distinct business

---

[8] Maryville University, Traditional Types of Business Models, online.maryville.edu.
[9] Wiener et al. (2020). Big-data business models: A critical literature review and multiperspective research framework, *Journal of Information Technology*, 35(1) 66–91.

models. Firstly, there are data users' models, which pertain to companies that leverage extensive data to streamline their business operations or create products and services. Secondly, there are business models for companies that collect, organize, and sell data to users. Lastly, there are business models for data facilitators who enable other companies to utilize data by providing the necessary infrastructure or analytics as a service.

On the other hand, Weber et al. (2021)[10] have categorized business models into four types. The first type is AI-charged product/service providers, who offer products or services that come equipped with pre-trained AI models. The second type is AI development facilitators, who primarily focus on assisting their customers in developing AI-related projects. The third type is data analytics providers, who concentrate on integrating and analyzing vast amounts of data. Lastly, there are deep-technology researchers, who are engaged in advancing the frontier of AI invention, development, and applications.

To summarize, considering the aforementioned research and other findings, business models for companies focused on AI can be categorized into three groups: (1) AI infrastructure providers, (2) AI application providers, and (3) AI adopters. The fees or prices charged to users are typically established by the respective AI product or service provider.

Venture Financing[11]

Entrepreneurs often require funding to support the establishment and expansion of their ventures. When pursuing capital for their promising ventures, entrepreneurs typically approach three primary sources of significant investment: (1) venture capitalists, (2) angel investors, and

---

[10] Weber, Michael et al (2021). AI Startup Business Models: Key Characteristics and Directions for Entrepreneurship Re-search, Business Information Systems Engineering, 64(1), 91-109.
[11] See, for example, Ferrati, Francesco and Muffatto, Moreno (2021). Reviewing equity investors' funding crite-ria: a comprehensive classification and research agenda, *Venture Capital*, https://www.tandfonline.com/doi/abs/10.1080/13691066.2021.1883211; Nunes, Jose C. et al (2014). Which criteria matter most in the evaluation of venture capital investments? *Journal of Small Business and Enterprise Development*, https://www.emerald.com/insight/content/doi/10.1108/JSBED-10-2013-0165/full/html?src=recsys&mobileUi=0; Hall, John and Hofer, Charles W. (1993). Venture capitalists' decision criteria in new venture evaluation, *Journal of Business Venturing*, 8(42), 25-42, https://www.sciencedirect.com/science/article/abs/pii/088390269390009T.

(3) other investors, including individuals and institutions. Regardless of the funding source, potential investors rigorously evaluate funding proposals based on strict guidelines, industry standards, and specific criteria for granting approval. The following outlines some of the requirements that entrepreneurs must meet:

Entrepreneurial team

The Entrepreneurial team is of utmost importance to investors, who carefully assess their relevant industry experience and track record. They value a team with a visionary outlook, capable of effectively navigating environmental challenges and competition. Moreover, investors seek out teams with the expertise to identify opportunities and the skills necessary to execute strategic plans for the business venture.

Product and service

To ensure success, the product or service being provided, or planned to be provided, should possess distinctiveness, value, and appeal to a significant and expanding customer base. Distinctiveness signifies either a lack of competition or the likelihood of minimal competition within the market. Product distinctiveness can manifest through factors such as size, shape, color, or other specifications. Service distinctiveness may be observed regarding swift delivery, convenience, competitive pricing, or similar attributes. Moreover, the offering should hold value for customers, ensuring sustained and increasing demand over the long term.

Market

The magnitude of the target market and its growth rates also hold great significance for prospective investors. Venture capitalists and other investors aim to secure their investments and generate suitable returns. Entrepreneurs who pursue venture financing must showcase in their business plans how the market's size and projected growth will ensure profitability, competitiveness, and sustainability for their ventures. Expanding markets are particularly associated with emerging industries and groundbreaking technologies.

Financial Outlook

Ensuring a continuous flow of revenue is crucial for the long-term viability of any business endeavor. It is important to distinguish between revenue (income) and earnings (profit). Revenue represents the total amount of money a company receives or generates within a specific timeframe, such as a year. Conversely, earnings are calculated by subtracting total expenses from the total revenue. When creating an entrepreneurial business plan, it is essential to clearly identify the sources of expected revenue in a detailed manner, as well as project the associated costs. Typically, this analysis is conducted for a three-year period. Careful consideration and attention to detail are necessary to determine the projected profitability of the venture accurately.

Other factors

Emerging entrepreneurial startups are anticipated to bring forth groundbreaking products and services, supported by AI-driven technologies, offering a compelling value proposition. These startups need to outline a well-defined exit strategy, aiming to either transition into publicly-owned entities or be acquired by a third party. Additionally, they should possess a scalable business model to foster their growth as globally-oriented enterprises.

Digital Transformation

Embracing digital transformation is essential for entrepreneurs and businesses to stay competitive and attain enduring success. It involves harnessing digital tools like data analytics and other transformative technologies to gain insights and enhance ventures' performance. Entrepreneurs must adopt a growth and agile mindset to navigate the constantly evolving digital landscape. By embracing digital transformation, entrepreneurs can cultivate a culture of innovation and resilience, unlocking the full potential of their businesses and creating a future where the possibilities are boundless.

What is digital transformation? According to Salesforce,[12] it "is the process of using digital technologies to create new - or modify existing - business processes, culture, or experiences to meet changing business and

---

[12] Salesforce, https://www.salesforce.com

market requirements". The company adds that digital transformation is changing how business gets done, and the process is leading to the

creation of new businesses. Business digitization can increase efficiency, boost margins, enhance customer relationships, and improve competitive advantage.

On the other hand, Dynatrace[13] indicates that digital transformation is an approach to changing how a business enterprise leverages technology, people, and processes to improve performance and embrace new business models. The spectrum of digital products and services is vast and expanding rapidly. It encompasses many offerings, including eBooks, photography, software programs, web-based applications, graphic arts, online courses, and music and audio content.

Digital technologies encompass various tools and machines that facilitate the gathering, examination, storage, and dissemination of data and other forms of information. These technologies include computers, blockchain, artificial intelligence, cloud computing, big data, mobile devices, and the Internet.

Benefits of Digital Transformation[14]

Numerous writers concur that the advent of digital transformation has had a significant impact on various aspects, including the creation and delivery of products and services, organizational activities and performance, and customer acquisition and retention. The primary advantages resulting from this transformation can be summarized as follows:

1. Increased productivity of the workforce and improved organizational performance.

2. Creation of a flexible and agile organization.

---

[13] Dynatrace, https://www.dynatrace.com.
[14] See, for example, https://www.techtarget.com/searchcio/tip/Top-10-digital-transformation-benefits-for-business; Lind, Mark (2018). Taking an Open-Systems Approach to PLM Gives Manufacturers Digital Transformation Advantages, *Manufacturing Engineering*, 161(1), 24, 26-28; Irsak, Mario and Barilovic, Zlatko (February 2023). Digital Transformation Project in a Function of Raising Competitive Advantage, *Economic and Social Development Book or Proceeding*.

3. Enhanced decision-making processes and better outcomes due to the availability of real-time critical data.

4. Heightened customer satisfaction resulting from improved communication and service.

5. Accelerated and more reliable processes through the automation of repetitive tasks.

6. Elevated workforce satisfaction due to automation, decentralized authority, and improved opportunities for professional development.

7. Enhanced security of operations and communication systems through implementing anti-spam measures and protection against unauthorized use of intellectual and other digital assets.

8. Greater adaptability to environmental changes.

9. Reduced costs and improved profitability.

An example, Nike reportedly utilizes AI to drive its Personal Recommendation Engine, facilitating customers in discovering the ideal shoes tailored to their requirements. The company leverages blockchain technology to track the authenticity of its products while employing extensive data analysis and big data techniques to gain insights into customer behavior and trends. Furthermore, Nike harnesses the power of cloud computing to store and process data efficiently, enabling seamless scalability of its operations. Lastly, Nike prioritizes cybersecurity measures to safeguard its data against potential cyber threats.

Dimensions, Enablers, and Propositions

Table 2 below summarizes the dimensions, enablers, and propositions of digital transformation as outlined by Samsung, Inc. The table highlights that digital data, connectivity, automation, and customer access are the key pillars of digital transformation. Additionally, it demonstrates the limitless realm of business opportunities within this domain, offering entrepreneurs and businesses various possibilities. These opportunities include the following:

- Inventing and innovating in the field of digital transformation.

- Developing and offering digital products and services.

- Selling or exchanging digital products and services.

- Renting or sharing digital products and services.

Providing consultation, training, and publishing in the field.

Table 2

Digital transformation: the enablers and propositions

Digital transformation	Enablers	Propositions
Digital data	Robotics	E-commerce
Connectivity	Additive manufacturing	Autonomous vehicles
Automation	Social networks	Fourth party logistics
Customer access	Mobile internet applications	Infotainment
	Broadband	Drones
	Cloud computing	Remote maintenance
	Internet of Things	Pure digital products
	Big data	Smart factory
	Wearable	Predictive maintenance
		Demand forecast
		Data-based routing

Source: Digital data transformation, Samsung White Paper, 2020, as reported by Mishra, Shrutika, and Tripathi, A. R. (2021), *Journal of Innovation and Entrepreneurship,* 10(18).

Assessment Need for Digital Transformation

When it comes to evaluating the necessity of digital transformation, both startups and established companies follow a specific methodology. Consulting firms commonly suggest an approach that entails understanding the organization's technological strengths and weaknesses, including the technical capabilities of their workforce, as well as the strategic vision and aspirations of the leadership. The goal of this analysis is to create a comprehensive digital transformation strategy that improves operational efficiency, profitability, and competitive advantage.

The assessment encompasses several factors, such as the company's offerings (products/services), market position, digital technologies employed by key competitors, and business strategy. Digital transformation is a broad process that encompasses all aspects of the company's operations, communication systems, and distribution channels. Once the assessment is complete, a transformation plan is formulated, detailing the necessary technologies, training programs, and funding requirements for the implementation phase. Initially, a pilot program may be executed, and upon successful outcomes, a fullfledged program can be implemented and evaluated for its effectiveness in achieving the desired transformation goals.

Summary

Entrepreneurship is an ongoing journey involving a series of actions from venture establishment to culmination. The objective is to attain a competitive advantage and reasonable return on investment by offering unique products or services that create value for customers. Factors such as political stability and a population inclined towards entrepreneurship contribute to the rise of entrepreneurial firms in the United States. Government support through legislation, grants, and loan guarantees also plays a significant role.

AI entrepreneurs actively pursue ventures that utilize artificial intelligence (AI) for tasks requiring human intelligence, assuming higher risks and potential rewards. US entrepreneurial companies are shifting their business models to focus on deploying AI technology and hiring skilled workforces, aligning with changing market sentiment and international business trends. Entrepreneurs seek funding from venture capitalists, angel investors, and other sources, with potential investors carefully evaluating proposals based on guidelines and industry standards.

Digital transformation is crucial for entrepreneurs and businesses to stay competitive and achieve lasting success. By leveraging digital tools like data analytics, entrepreneurs gain insights and enhance venture performance. Adopting a growth mindset and embracing digital transformation allows entrepreneurs to foster innovation and resilience and unlock the full potential of their ventures.

Questions

1. Define the concept of entrepreneurship.

2. Explore the parallels and distinctions between traditional entrepreneurs and AI entrepreneurs.

3. Describe the various funding options available for entrepreneurial endeavors.

4. Provide a comprehensive explanation of the key characteristics associated with digital transformation.

Chapter 2

Introduction to Business Strategies

"Strategy is a fancy word for coming up with a long-term plan and putting it into action"

Ellie Pidot

Chapter Objectives

- Gain an understanding of the concept of strategy.

- Outline the significance of business strategies.

- Discuss the phases involved in the strategic management model.

- Provide a detailed explanation of the vision statement for the venture.

Learning about strategies is fascinating because they are plans that enable organizations to grow and flourish. Strategies are essential for organizations of all sizes, industries, and economic sectors, whether they are for profit or not-for-profit, domestic or international, resource-rich or resource-poor. Well-crafted and well-executed viable strategies can pave the way for organizational progress and sustainability. To navigate through the challenging environments of venture creation, development, and profitability, entrepreneurs and other business-minded individuals need to advance their knowledge and skills of business strategies.

The creation and effective management of strategic entrepreneurial companies require the implementation of winning strategies to ensure ongoing success and prevent failure. Entrepreneurial companies vary in many aspects such as their rate of growth, leadership experience, organizational structure, resource endowment, workforce skills, and the types of goods and/or services they offer. Additionally, they differ in terms of target markets, including local, national, or international markets, and target customers such as the young, elderly, or middle-income individuals. As a result, entrepreneurial strategies vary in complexity and type.

What's Strategy?

Strategy can be defined as a plan of action, or simply a plan. However, in a broader sense, it serves as a long-term guide to activities and a clear roadmap that helps a company achieve its strategic goals and objectives. The field of business strategy is comprised of three interconnected stages: strategy formation (also known as strategy analysis), strategy execution, and strategy evaluation. Despite their interrelated nature, strategies are not developed in isolation; they are created and executed within the context of a company's internal and external environment. This environment consists of various factors that collectively influence the company's performance and success. The analysis of the environment, coupled with the three stages mentioned earlier, is commonly known as the strategic management process, strategic management model, or strategic planning.

On the other hand, strategic entrepreneurship involves the pursuit of superior performance through the pursuit of opportunities and exploiting them. By effectively integrating strategic entrepreneurship and innovation, both small and large firms can enhance their potential to generate wealth[15]. Meanwhile, according to Paek and Lee (2018), strategic entrepreneurship entails several key components, such as environmental screening, opportunity identification and capture, strategic flexibility, entrepreneurial orientation, and organizational learning[16].

---

[15] Ketchen Jr., David J. et all (2008). Strategic Entrepreneurship, Collaborative Innovation, and Wealth Creation, Strategic Entrepreneurial Journal, 1(3/4), 371-385.

[16] Paek, Byunqioo and Lee, Heesang (2018). Strategic Entrepreneurship and Competitive Advantage of Estab-lished Firms: Evidence from the Digital TV Industry, *International Entrepreneurship and Management Journal*, 14(4), 883-925.

Are Strategies Needed?

What is the significance of deploying business strategies, and why are strategies crucial to the success of a business? Undoubtedly, there are numerous advantages for both entrepreneurial and established companies to utilize business strategies as they strive to survive and compete. The benefits of effective business strategies include:

- Enabling companies to achieve their goals and objectives in areas such as innovation, growth, and profitability.

- Assisting companies in expanding their market reach by attracting and retaining new customers.

- Providing guidance to companies in their recruitment, training, and professional development programs for their employees.

- Helping companies with capital allocation and budgeting.

- Bringing discipline to the decision-making process and project prioritization.

How to Create a Business Strategy?

To develop a business strategy, a number of interrelated steps are involved that comprise the strategic management process or strategic planning. These steps can be categorized as follows:

- Defining the business concept and model, particularly for a startup enterprise.

- Carrying out an analysis of both internal and external environments, also known as a situational analysis.

- Establishing the company's vision and mission.

- Setting specific goals and objectives.

- Creating a strategy.

- Assessing the effectiveness of the strategy.

Business Concept and Business Model

When embarking on a startup venture, entrepreneurs need to create a business concept that serves as a foundation for their vision statement. The concept outlines the intended line of business, target customers, and market, summarizing the initial idea behind the venture's creation. As the concept is usually refined and further articulated during the development of the business plan and market analysis, venture capitalists, angel investors, and other investors typically expect entrepreneurs to provide a full justification and explanation for their startup ventures when seeking seed money or growth financing.

The following are examples of business concepts:

- Starting a business venture to produce and sell athletic shoes in the United States.

- Establishing a venture to manufacture and sell electronic toys for children.

- Creating a daycare center in Washington, D.C. to care for children under the age of 4.

- Setting up an all-purpose printing company to serve individual customers and businesses worldwide.

The business model, on the other hand, pertains to the capacity of a venture to yield profits in the future. To put it differently, the projected profitability of the venture is evaluated by computing the variance between the estimated cost and projected revenue within a specific time frame. It goes without saying that if the business model demonstrates that the venture is incapable of generating profits in the future, say within the first two years of operation, then endeavors to pursue the planned startup must be discontinued. It is crucial to bear in mind that the cost and revenue estimations of the venture are established on a comprehensive market analysis and examination.

Market Opportunities

Market opportunities are economic prospects that encourage entrepreneurs and other com-panies to invest capital and resources in new ventures or expand existing operations to reach new markets and consumers, with the aim of achieving a reasonable rate of return on their investment. According to Dictionary.com, an opportunity is "a situation or condition favorable for the attainment of a goal."

There are various sources of information available about market opportunities. One crucial source of information is the entrepreneurs themselves, who have valuable knowledge due to their education, work experience, familiarity with certain goods and services, and hobbies. Other valuable sources of information include magazines, newspapers, radio, television, social media, the Internet, and ChatGPT.

Furthermore, the North American Industry Classification System (NAICS) is an invaluable reference source for the U.S. economy. NAICS is a statistical system specifically designed for national data gathering and reporting. It classifies all economic activities within the country into various categories and subcategories. By familiarizing oneself with NAICS's key components and understanding the spending on each component, one can gain insights into the economic size of various sectors, industries, and subindustries, as well as the opportunities they offer. Table 1 below provides a breakdown of the NAICS components.

The table illustrates that business opportunities can be found in any of the twenty aggregate sectors of the U.S. economy, which collectively comprise 1,012 6-digit industries. Additionally, the table highlights that each sector includes numerous subsectors or industries. For example, sector 51, which pertains to information, comprises six primary subsectors:

- Motion Pictures and Sound Recording Industries
- Publishing Industries
- Broadcasting and Content Providers
- Telecommunications
- Computing Infrastructure Providers, Data Processing, Webhosting, and Related Services
- Web Services Portals, Libraries, Archives, and Other Information Services.

Additionally, each of the aforementioned subsectors is further categorized into smaller subsectors. For example, within the Publishing Industries sector, there are 14 distinct industries, including but not limited to newspaper publishing, book publishing, greeting card publishing, and software publishing. It is essential to highlight that the main objective of delving into the NAICS is to assist entrepreneurs in precisely identifying the target sector, industry, and sub-industry of their intended business operations. Accurately identifying the company's business domain will aid in conducting market research, creating a business plan, and securing venture funding.

Table 1

2022 North American Industry Classification System (NAICS)

Sector	Name	Total 6-digit in-dustries
11	Agriculture, Forestry, Fishing, and Hunting	64
21	Mining, Quarrying, and Oil and Gas Extraction	21
22	Utilities	14
23	Construction	31
31-33	Manufacturing	346
42	Wholesale Trade	69
44-45	Retail Trade	57
48-49	Transportation and Warehousing	57
51	Information	29
52	Finance and Insurance	35
53	Real Estate and Rental and Leasing	24
54	Professional, Scientific, and technical Services	49
55	Management of Companies and Enterprises	3
56	Administrative and Support and Waste Management and Remediation Services	44
61	Educational Services	17
62	Healthcare and Social Assistance	39
71	Arts, Entertainment, and Recreation	25
72	Accommodation and Food Services	15
81	Other Services (except Public Administration)	44
92	Public Administration	29
Total		1012

Source: Executive Office of the President, Office of Management and Budget, https://www.census.gov/naics/reference_files_tools/2022_NAICS_Manual.pdf.

It's important to recognize that some industries in the United States, like the fast-food industry, have an abundance of companies, leading to intense competition. To succeed in such a fiercely competitive setting, an entrepreneur's business endeavor must be truly groundbreaking. This entails introducing innovative strategies in product offerings, delivery, pricing, location, and other areas.

Vision Statement

As per the Oxford Languages dictionary definition, vision refers to the ability to imagine or plan the future with creativity and wisdom. In the realm of entrepreneurial business, vision entails envisioning market opportunities, creating new products, launching ventures, and anticipating potential profits. Vision represents the ultimate strategic goal for any company or venture.

Entrepreneurs aspire to reap rewards for their contributions and expertise by creating employment opportunities, investing resources, generating wealth, and contributing to the national income of their country.

The vision for a startup venture is subject to variation based on the entrepreneur's personal preferences, business acumen, available capital, confidence in new products, market potential potential, and other critical factors. The venture's vision and business concept are closely intertwined notions that must be aligned. Once the vision statement is finalized, it should be incorporated into the business plan, phrased with care, and no more than two sentences. Statements that are unclear or contain too many ideas may perplex readers.

Examples of vision statements include:

Software Company: "Our vision is to become the foremost provider of internet security services."

Daycare Center: "Our vision is to provide young children with an enjoyable daily life."

Information Service Company: "We aim to provide customers with the most dependable daily economic and market updates."

Consulting Company: "Our vision is to aid small business owners through strategy development, training, and technical assistance."

7-Eleven, Inc: Be the first choice for convenience, anytime, anywhere.

Apple, Inc: We believe that we are on face of the earth to make great products, and that's not changing.

Bank of America: To be the world's finest financial service company.

General Motor, Inc: To be the automotive industry in creating a world with zero crashes, zero emissions, and zero congestions.

The Vision for the Venture

As mentioned earlier, an entrepreneur's vision for their business is a statement that looks ahead and captures the essence of the venture, its value proposition for potential customers, and its long-term goals. Crafting a well-thought-out vision statement has several important benefits:

- It helps the entrepreneur stay focused on the mission and objectives of the venture.

- It gives employees a clear sense of direction and purpose in their roles and responsibilities.

- It conveys the company's values and dedication to its customers.

- It can assist in securing funding by outlining the business's potential and prospects.

- It inspires and motivates the workforce to accomplish the venture's objectives.

- It acts as a unifying force, promoting agreement and alignment among the entrepreneurial team on strategic matters.

Summary

The success of entrepreneurial ventures and other companies is crucial for the national economy. To remain competitive, these entities must implement well-researched and well-developed business strategies. These strategies serve as organizational roadmaps that need to be formulated, evaluated, and executed. Additionally, it's essential to analyze and evaluate the outcomes of strategy implementation to determine whether strategic change or modification is necessary.

Formulating a business strategy requires investigating both internal and external factors, such as workforce skills and competition. A venture's vision, which represents its ultimate reason for existence, should be communicated in a clear, concise statement to inform both employees and outsiders about the company's intended future destination and outlook.

To gain critical information about the U.S. economy and market opportunities, it's important to review the North American Industry Classification System (NAICS).

Questions

1. Define the concept of business strategy.

2. Analyze the significance of strategies for corporations such as Walmart.

3. As a business consultant, craft a vision statement for a computer training startup with a staff of 15.

4. Elaborate on the advantages of knowing NAICS.

Notes

Mishra and Mohanty (2022)[17] pointed out that authors have approached the meaning of strategy from different viewpoints as (a) a vehicle to achieve the firm's long-term objectives, (b) a mechanism for coping with environmental change, (c) a tool to finding a match between the firm's resources and market opportunities, and (d) as a means of achieving the firm's competitive advantage. The authors emphasized that strategy is viewed as a planning process.

Moreover, Bayo-Moriones et al (2021)[18] pointed out that a clearly defined strategy can direct the company's workforce efforts and actions toward the accomplishment of its strategic goals and objectives.

[17] Mishra, Subrat P. and Mohanty, Brajarai (2022). Approaches to Strategy Formulations: A Content Analysis of Definitions of Strategy, *Journal of Management and Organization*, 28(6), 1133-1160.
[18] Bayo-Moriones, Alberto et al (2021). Business Strategy, Performance Appraisal and Organizational Results, *Personnel Review*, 50(2), 515-534.

Chapter 3

GUIDELINES TO BUSINESS STRATEGIES FORMULATION

> "Leasers establish the vision for the future and
> set the strategy for getting there"
>
> John P. Kotter

Chapter Objectives

- Comprehend the significance of a company's mission and its interpretation.

- Explain the distinction between a company's vision and mission.

- Attain proficiency in the process of strategy formulation.

- Acquire knowledge of investigating a company's internal environment.

To commence the strategic planning process for a startup venture, the initial step involves the formulation of its strategy. This encompasses the creation of the venture's vision, developing a mission statement, defining goals and objectives, evaluating alternative strategies, and eventually choosing a desired strategy or embarking on strategic initiatives. The preliminary stage of strategy formulation requires an assessment of the venture's internal dynamics and external factors.

Strategic Planning Cycle

The initial phase of strategic planning involves the development of a strategy (items 1 through 5). This process sets the foundation for the entire strategic planning cycle, which encompasses items 1 through 7.

1. Establish the venture's vision.

2. Craft a mission statement that aligns with the vision.

3. Conduct a SWOT analysis, examining both the venture's internal state and external circumstances to identify its strengths, weaknesses, opportunities, and threats.

4. Determine a strategy or initiative based on the SWOT analysis findings.

5. Assess the feasibility and practicality of the chosen strategy or initiatives.

6. Put the selected strategy or initiatives into action.

7. Evaluate the outcomes of the strategy and make necessary adjustments if needed.

The Mission

Thompson et al. (2020)[19] explain that a company's mission statement defines its current business scope, purpose, and identity as an organization. In contrast, a company's vision statement outlines its future aspirations and outlook. While the mission statement centers on the present operations and market focus of the company, the vision statement articulates its long-term designation.

The following are examples of mission statements:

Software Company

We take great pride in being among the leading software companies in the Washington metropolitan region with regard to Internet security. Our primary emphasis is on monitoring the Internet security of our

---

[19] Thompson, Arthur et at (2020). *Crafting and Executing Strategy*, New York: NY, McGraw-Hill Publications, Inc.

clients, perpetually thwarting transaction safety breaches, and safeguarding communication between clients and the external world. You can depend on our punctual, trustworthy, and customer-oriented services.

Daycare Center

At our daycare center, our unwavering commitment is to offer exceptional care to young children all over the United States. Our main focus is on creating a comfortable and safe environment that provides ample opportunities for human interaction and a secure space for children. Our mission is to nurture the growth of each child's personality and cognitive abilities, and we achieve this through our well-designed, contemporary daycare centers.

Information Service Company

Our commitment as an information provider is to deliver valuable insights to our global business clients. Our emphasis is on delivering daily updates of precise, pertinent, and up-to-date information, including data, news, and critical facts about market trends and developments. Our mission is to empower our clients with the knowledge necessary to make informed decisions and stay ahead of the competition.

Consulting Company

Our consulting firm is dedicated to delivering superior consultation and services to small businesses in our local community. Our expertise spans across various functional areas, including strategic recommendations, organizational structure design, workforce training, and technical assistance. We are firmly committed to ensuring client satisfaction and retention, which motivates us to provide exceptional results that cater to the specific needs of every business we assist.

Bank of America

To help make financial lives better by connecting clients and communities to the resources they need to be successful.

Starbucks

To inspire and nurture the human spirit – one person, one cup, and one neighborhood at a time.

Apple, Inc.

Bringing the best user experience to its customers through innovative hardware, software and services.

General Motor, Inc.

To earn customers for life by building brands that inspire passion and loyalty through not only breakthrough technologies but also be serving and improving the communities in which we live and work around the world.

As indicated earlier, a mission statement should be comprehensive and unambiguous, comprising one to three sentences. An effective statement should encompass at least three fundamental elements, namely:

- The business domain of the company (such as consulting);

- The target market (such as the United States); and

- The target customers (such as young children).

The mission statement of a company, like its vision, serves multiple purposes, such as:

- Identifying the company's business, industry, target market, and customer base.

- Providing employees with a framework for understanding the company's business field and operations.

- Attracting qualified technical and managerial personnel to join the company.

- Introducing the company to stakeholders, trade associations, government agencies, and the public.

- Aiding the company in unifying the efforts of its employees towards achieving its strategic goals and vision.

Goals [20] and Objectives

A goal in the business context refers to a target or desired outcome resulting from a series of deliberate organizational decisions. It typically encompasses a broad statement of intention. For instance, here are some examples of goals that XYZ furniture company may have:

- Boost the company's revenue.

- Improve product quality.

- Expand the company's market share.

- Establish a global presence.

- Integrate artificial intelligence (AI) technologies in business operations.

The following are additional goals:

Apple, Inc.
To create products that enrich people's daily life.

T-Mobile
Our goal is to offer the best network experience and the best value.

Ford, Motor, Inc.
To help build a better world, where every person is free to move and pursue their dreams.

On the flip side, objectives can be viewed as desired targets that convert goals into measurable outcomes through a sequence of actions. The following are examples of objectives:

- Boost the company's revenue by 20% before the conclusion of the upcoming year.

- Within six months, we aim to enhance the quality of our products by integrating AI technologies and recruiting four highly skilled

---

[20] Oxford Languages dictionary defines goal as "the object of a person's ambition or effort; an aim or desired result".

employees.

- Our objective is to increase our market share by investing an additional $100,000 in the promotional budget each year and hiring new sales personnel.

- We plan to engage an international consultant to facilitate the company's establishment of business contacts in Europe, with a target completion date of two years.

- To leverage machine learning and other AI technologies, we aim to hire two software engineers within four months to guide our efforts.

It is essential to ensure that the vision, mission, goals, and objectives are aligned with each other and the business strategy of the venture. For example, if the vision is to achieve market dominance, the goals and objectives should be in line with this vision to guarantee successful attainment. Failure to align these aspects may impede the implementation of an effective strategy and, consequently, retard organizational performance[21].

Internal Analysis

The primary objective of an internal business investigation is to assess its strengths and weaknesses. This involves two key decisions: (i) mitigating or eliminating weaknesses and (ii) aligning the enterprise's strengths with available market opportunities while factoring in its weaknesses and external threats. To conduct a SWOT analysis effectively, it's crucial to focus on significant factors and limit the number of factors to no more than ten for each of the strengths, weaknesses, opportunities, and threats.

The following are some internal factors to consider when conducting a SWOT analysis:

- Leadership and Management: This refers to the quality of leadership and managerial competencies within a company, as

---

[21] The term performance is generally used to indicate profitability, market share, productivity, return on investment, or other company accomplishments or lack of it.

well as the effectiveness of the labor skills and team dynamics.

- Technology and Equipment: This encompasses the use of machines, computers, tools, and other related equipment to support the company's operations and processes.

- Production and Operations Efficiency: This is the ability of the company to produce and operate, minimizing waste and maximizing productivity efficiently.

- Cost of Inputs: This includes the cost of labor and materials required for the company's operations.

- Product Quality, Reliability, and Delivery: This refers to the quality, reliability, and timely delivery of the company's products or services.

- Facilities: This includes the availability and quality of facilities that are required for the company's operations.

- Capital and Financing: This encompasses the amount of capital and the sources of finance available to the company to support its operations and growth.

- Customer Retention: This refers to the ability of the company to attract and retain its customers and maintain customer loyalty.

- Company Reputation: This is the perception of the company by its stakeholders, including customers, employees, investors, and the general public.

- Intellectual Property: This includes patents, trademarks, and other forms of intellectual property that the company owns.

- Company Location: This refers to the location of the company and its impact on its operations and market positioning.

- Diversification: This refers to the extent to which the company has diversified its operations and investments.

- Strategic Planning: This encompasses the company's strategic plans and its ability to implement them effectively.

- Stakeholder Relationships: This refers to the company's relationships with its stakeholders, including employees, suppliers, investors, and other partners.

Table 1 below shows the strengths and weaknesses of XYZ Modern Furniture Company

Table 1
XYZ Modern Furniture Company: Internal Assessment
(Strengths and weaknesses)

Strengths (S)	Weaknesses (W)
1. Capital in excess of current needs. 2. Products of superior quality. 3. Competitive advantage in the market. 4. Marketing expertise. 5. Technical and managerial proficiencies. 6. Strong customer loyalty. 7. Effective leadership. 8. Successful formulation of strategic plans. 9. National recognition of trademark. 10. State-of-the-art warehouses.	1. Insufficient sales personnel. 2. Limited experience in exporting. 3. confusing company goals. 4. Escalating internal disputes among senior staff. 5. Internal reluctance to embrace change. 6. Outdated company website. 7. Outdated computers and software. 8. Lack of proficiency in utilizing artificial intelligence (AI) in company operations. 9. Excessive monitoring and control measures. 10. Recent reduction in workforce professional development program due to funding cuts.

Source. Hypothetical internal analysis.

Summary

The strategic management process begins with strategy formulation, where a variety of decisions and activities are undertaken to create effective strategies. This stage involves developing and communicating the vision and mission of the venture to stakeholders. The mission statement outlines the company's business domain, target market, and target customers, while goals and objectives are established to align with the overall strategy.

To create successful strategies, it is important to conduct an analysis of the internal and external environment of the company or venture. One commonly used approach is SWOT analysis, which identifies the strengths, weaknesses, opportunities, and threats of the company. This analysis helps to leverage strengths to capitalize on opportunities and address internal weaknesses and external threats. It is recommended to investigate a maximum of 10 factors for each SWOT component.

After the strategies are developed through SWOT analysis, they should be evaluated to ensure they are suitable for implementation. This evaluation process involves answering questions such as whether the strategy aligns with the venture's goals and objectives.

Questions

1. What is the significance of a mission statement?

2. Create a mission statement for a company of your preference.

3. What are some internal factors that impact the performance of department stores?

4. Elucidate the goal of conducting a SWOT analysis for a company.

Notes

An intriguing observation within the realm of strategy formulation pertains to the classification of business organizations by certain authors, who divide them into two primary categories and further subdivide them into ten distinct groups, as outlined below: (See, for example, Miller, Danny and Friesen, Peter S. (1978). Archetypes of Strategy Formulation, *Management Science,* 24(9), 921-933):

A. Successful archetypes which include:

- Adaptive firm under moderate challenge.

- Adaptive firm in a very challenging environment.

- Dominant firm.

- Giant under fire.

- Entrepreneurial conglomerate.

- Innovator.

B. Failure archetypes which include:

- Impulsive firm.

- Stagnant bureaucracy.

- Headless giant.

- Aftermath.

Chapter 4

THE EXTERNAL ENVIRONMENT AND STRATEGY DEVELOPMENT

"Each one chooses his own path to come in contact with the external world,
I chose to merge with the environment"

Liu Bolin

Chapter Objectives

- Gain an understanding of the need for external analysis.

- Provide examples of external factors.

- Discuss the process of strategy implementation.

- Outline the criteria used for evaluating strategies

In the preceding chapter, we delved into the analysis of the internal environment of the venture. In this chapter, we will focus on the venture's external environment. By combining both investigations, we can develop alternative strategies or strategic initiatives, as exemplified later in this chapter.

Examining the External Environment

There are several external factors that can significantly impact the performance of a business venture in different ways. These factors include, but are not limited to:

- The country's gross domestic product (GDP).

- Expenditures made by the government.

- Imports and exports of goods and services.

- Spending by consumers and businesses.

- Cultural forces, including beliefs and values.

- Technological advancements, such as machine learning, ChatGPT, and other innovations.

- Political environment, encompassing stability and internal unrest.

- Social forces, such as unemployment and poverty levels.

- Level of domestic and international competition.

- National inflation rates and interest rates.

- Global conflicts, such as wars and sanctions.

Although the variables mentioned above have a significant impact on a venture's performance, it is essential to focus primarily on the relevant factors that affect the industry in which the venture operates during external analysis. For instance, if the venture deals with domestic banking activities, inflation and interest rates hold more importance than cultural forces or global conflicts. Conversely, if the venture belongs to the fast-food industry, consumer spending and competition are more relevant than government expenditures or the political environment. The primary concern is that while developing a SWOT analysis, external factors that have a direct impact on both the venture and its industry should be included.

Table 2 presented below is a hypothetical example of external factors that affect the market performance of XYZ Modern Furniture Company.

Table 2

XYZ Modern Furniture Company

(Opportunities and threats)

Opportunities (O)	Threats (T)
1. The economy of the United States is experiencing growth. 2. A survey has shown that there is consumer interest in the company's products internationally. 3. There is an increase in the rate of construction for both residential homes and office buildings in the country. 4. The population of the United States is rapidly growing. 5. A recent agreement made with an international supplier has the potential to reduce the cost of production. 6. The company has attracted interest from external parties looking to acquire it. 7. An international furniture exhibition is scheduled to take place in a European country next year.	1. New domestic competitors have emerged. 2. The cost of both materials and labor is on the rise. 3. Companies are encountering higher tax rates. 4. There is an increasing expectation that the country may soon enter a recession. 5. Foreign furniture suppliers have imitated the style and design of the company's furniture. 6. The country is currently undergoing a high inflation rate which could potentially decrease consumer spending on furniture. 7. There has been a recent tariff increase on imported lumber from Canada. 8. There is an anticipated negative shift toward corporate America in Congress.

Source. Hypothetical example for illustration.

Developing Strategic Initiatives

Upon careful examination of the SWOT analysis results depicted in tables 1 and 2, several strategies or strategic initiatives can be formulated {strengths (S), weaknesses (W), opportunities (O), and threats (T)}:

- Constructing new production facilities (S1, O1, O2, and O4).

- Renovating the company's website (S1, W6).

- Recruiting the necessary sales force (S1, W7).

- Selling the company at a premium price (S2, S3, S6, and O6).

- Undertaking professional development programs (S1, S8, and W10).

- Hiring a consultant to assess managerial procedures and practices (S1, S7, W4, and W9).

- Exploring related product diversification (S1, S5, S7, T1, and T7).

This list serves as an example of potential actions that the company's leadership could consider. However, it is important to note that additional initiatives may also be generated from the SWOT analysis presented in tables 1 and 2. It is critical to emphasize that SWOT analysis should be utilized in the formulation of business strategies, as it is the first stage in the process of strategic planning to ensure the credibility and viability of the chosen course(s) of action.

As indicated earlier, strategic initiatives are developed by leveraging the strengths (S) and opportunities (O) of a company, while also addressing its weaknesses (W) and threats (T). For instance, the initial initiative above was formulated based on S1, which represents the availability of company capital as outlined in Table 1, and the existing opportunities (O1, O2, and O4). Initiatives should also aim to consider ways to mitigate weaknesses and threats.

The implementation of the selected initiative(s) depends on the entrepreneurs' vision, experience, resources, and market knowledge. Whichever initiative(s) is chosen, it needs to be evaluated before execution to avoid unnecessary costs and efforts.

In the context of external analysis of strategy formulation, Michael Porter of Harvard University introduced a model known as the Five Forces that shape industry competition model[22], which includes:

- Rivalry among existing competitors

- Threats of new entrants

- Bargaining power of buyers

- Threat of substitute products or services

- Bargaining power of suppliers

---

[22] Porter, Michael (2008). The Five Competitive Forces That Shape Strategy, *Harvard Business Review*86(1), 78-93.

The model proposes that these forces have a direct impact on the performance of a business enterprise in the marketplace. To achieve a competitive advantage, a firm must develop competence in areas such as technology, productivity, human skills, and strategy.

Strategy Evaluation

In order to effectively evaluate a strategy or strategic initiative, it is crucial to consider a set of criteria. One approach to achieving this is by asking a series of questions such as:

1. Does the strategy align with the company's leadership vision?

2. Should the strategy be implemented currently or considered for the future?

3. Is the strategy feasible in terms of time, capital, effort, and other required resources?

4. Will the strategy contribute to the company's competitive advantage and profitability in the medium term, say within two to three years?

5. Is the strategy legally, socially, ethically, and financially sound?

6. Is the strategy within the company's risk tolerance level?

7. Is the strategy disruptive?

8. Does the strategy utilize appropriate technology?

Insufficient market research can result in costly strategic errors for businesses. Ian Kirk[23] mentioned several companies, including Ford, Coca-Cola, Sony, and Gap, that have fallen into this trap. In the case of Ford, reports indicate that the company invested $250 million and ten years in planning a new car called the "Edsel," which was launched in 1957. However, due to low sales and negative public reception, it was discontinued just two years later in 1959.

---

[23] Kirk, Ian, The Biggest Marketing Blunders of All Time (https://articles.bplans.com). Uploaded in March 2023.

Additionally, SVB Financial Group, the 14th largest financial institution in the United States with assets totaling $212 billion, failed in March 2023 due to disastrous managerial decisions made over a period of time. This led to the institution near bankruptcy and subsequent government takeover.

It is important to note that the process of building a strategy involves both art and science. The scientific aspect of strategy building is demonstrated through activities such as market research, statistical analysis, and the use of necessary AI-enabled software and hardware. On the other hand, the art of strategy building involves the application of experience, value judgment, and education by entrepreneurs and other decision-makers to determine the best strategy to pursue ultimately.

Summary

Strategy formulation marks the starting point of the strategic management process, encompassing a series of activities and decisions. For effective strategies, it is crucial to conduct a comprehensive analysis of the company's internal and external environment. The SWOT analysis is commonly employed to identify the strengths, weaknesses, opportunities, and threats of a company. Matching strengths with opportunities while considering internal weaknesses and external threats is crucial when devising strategies using SWOT. The generated strategies must undergo an evaluation to ensure their suitability and feasibility for implementation. Evaluation involves questioning whether the strategy aligns with the company's strategic goals and objectives.

Questions

1. What is the purpose of the external analysis?

2. What are some of the external factors that affect the performance of Universities?

3. Develop a SWOT analysis for a company of your choice.

4. What are the criteria that you may use to evaluate the current strategy of Starbucks?

Chapter 5

Types of Business Strategies

"Winning should be at the heart of every strategy".

A.G. Lafley & Roger L. Martin

Chapter Objectives

- Gain knowledge about the various types of business strategies.

- Comprehend the extent of the application of different strategies.

- Increase knowledge about the various methods utilized in implementing a differentiation strategy.

- Distinguish between defensive and offensive strategies.

Business strategies are diverse in type and scope, serving as a means to position a business enterprise to reach its desired goals. The strategies are designed to perform various functions and achieve distinct objectives. Several factors, including the size of the enterprise, resource availability, industry, competitive environment, expected return on investment, and top management risk tolerance influence the selection of a strategy. Regardless of the type of strategy or its scope, it must achieve the purpose for which it is deployed.

Types of Strategies

Business firms have employed various major strategies in the United States and other parts of the world for many decades. The strategies, which have unique variations, are categorized as either offensive (growth-oriented) or defensive.[24]

Offensive (growth-oriented) strategies include:

- Differentiation strategies.

- Integration strategies.

- Diversification strategies.

- Outsourcing strategies.

- Intensive Strategies.

- Joint venture strategies.

Defensive strategies include:

- Retrenchment strategies.

- Divestment strategies.

- Bankruptcy strategies.

On the other hand, there are four levels of strategies:

- Corporate strategies: These are primarily designed for multinational business enterprises and other large, diversified companies.

- Business strategies: These focus mainly on a single business or a division within a multinational business enterprise, which is the main subject of this book.

- Functional strategies: These encompass specific areas such as marketing and human resources.

- Operating strategies: These pertain to operational aspects like inventory control and maintenance.

---

[24] See for example, Thompson, Arthur et at (2020). Crafting and Executing Strategy, New York: NY, McGraw-Hill Publications, Inc; David, Fred R. and David, Forest R. (2017). Strategic Management, Boston: Massachusetts, Pear son Education, Inc; Rothaermel, Frank T (2015). Strategic Management, New York: NY, McGraw-Hill Education, Inc; Certo, Samuel C. and Certo, S. Travis (2014). Modern Management, Boston: Massachusetts, Pearson Educa-tion, Inc).

Differentiation Strategies

According to the Cambridge Dictionary, differentiation refers to "the act of showing or finding differences between things that are compared." In business, however, the term has come to indicate the uniqueness or distinctiveness of a product, service, trademark, talent, object, and the like. Companies utilize a differentiation strategy to influence consumers or end-users that what they offer, such as merchandise, is unique as compared to other products in the same class or group in the marketplace. These strategies often entail additional costs for the companies that deploy them. So, what are the benefits of such strategies?

The benefits of differentiation can be summarized as follows:

- Companies can charge premium prices for their unique products or services, leading to increased profits.

- Companies offering well-differentiated products and services can expand their market share, and secure customer loyalty.

- Differentiation can enhance a company's competitive advantage.

- Differentiation can improve a company's growth rate and chances of survival.

It is worth noting that numerous experts, among them Professor Michael Porter of Harvard University, are of the opinion that differentiation strategies can enable businesses to attain a competitive edge. Nevertheless, implementing excessive product differentiation could be a risky approach since customers may perceive the product or service as inappropriate for their requirements.

How Do Businesses Differentiate?

Product differentiation can be achieved through various means, including price, warranty, quality, and reputation, as well as physical characteristics such as size, length, and weight. Appearance is also a factor, encompassing design, color, and other aesthetic qualities. Additionally, convenience plays a role, with considerations like availability and speed of delivery being important factors. Finally, taste can be a key aspect for certain products such as coffee and beverages.

Similarly, services can be differentiated in various ways, including price, convenience, delivery, quality, reputation, and safety. By offering unique combinations of these factors, businesses can stand out from competitors and appeal to specific customer needs.

Examples of differentiation strategies:

7-Eleven, Inc. - convenience, accessibility.

Apple, Inc. - product design, service.

General Motor, Inc. - product design, quality.

Starbucks, Inc. - quality coffee, offering third-place experience (after home and office).

Audi - Hertrich and Mayrhofer[25] pointed out that the German company Audi, part of the Volkswagen Group, is enjoying unprecedented levels of success, particularly in the international marketplace. The company is one of the world leaders in the 'premium' car segment where it competes against other German companies like BMW and Mercedes. Audi has developed a differentiation strategy mainly based on the technology and quality of the services it offers. This strategic positioning is manifested by the slogan 'progress through technology'. The slogan is used by the brand in its communication campaigns throughout the world.

Integration Strategies

Business firms use various strategies to expand their market reach, achieve growth, and gain a competitive advantage. Integration strategies are a set of tools that aid firms in achieving these goals, and they can be classified into two groups: vertical integration and horizontal integration. Vertical integration, in turn, can be divided into two strategic initiatives: forward integration strategies and backward integration strategies.

When a firm pursues a forward strategy, its goal is to reach the final consumer directly, bypassing intermediary channels such as middlemen. An example of a forward integration strategy is when entrepreneurs create their products or offer services and sell them directly to customers

[25] Hertrich, Sylvia and Mayrhofer, Ulrike (2022). Strategy formulation at Audi, *IDEAS Working Paper Series, RePEc*, St. Louis.

via their own websites. Conversely, if an entrepreneur decides to create some or all of the raw materials input for a product and sell it on their website, they are using a backward integration strategy. In this case, the entrepreneur controls the source of supply of input materials and labor.

Horizontal integration happens when an entrepreneurial enterprise or firm acquires a competitor's business, such as Ford Motor Company buying General Motors Company (or vice versa). This strategic move is referred to as a horizontal integration strategy.

Implementing integration strategies, along with other growth-oriented strategies, involves inherent risks and uncertainties regarding their success. This is because of several factors, such as the higher cost of integration strategies compared to other feasible alternatives, challenges in aligning the culture, business practices, technology, or policies between the two entities, and the possibility of market conditions changing, which may render the chosen strategy unproductive.

Examples of integration strategies:

Walt Disney's acquisition of 21st Century Fox.

Facebook's (Meta Platform, Inc.) acquisition of WhatsApp.

Pfizer Inc. and Wyeth's merge.

Amazon's.com, Inc. acquisition of Whole Foods.

Diversification Strategies

Mid-sized and large firms, including multinational corporations (MNCs), often employ diversification strategies to expand their business operations from a single enterprise to a global multi-business enterprise. Successful diversification can result in increased profitability, market share, and rapid growth for firms. However, poor diversification decisions can be financially costly and may lead some firms to file for bankruptcy.

Diversification strategies can take two forms: related and unrelated. Related diversification occurs when an entrepreneurial firm acquires or creates a business that is related to its original (or core) line of business.

For example, an agricultural enterprise that specializes in bananas might acquire an apple orchard. The relatedness can be assessed based on whether the technology, raw materials, and labor skills used are the same, very similar, or entirely different in the acquiring and acquired firms.

Unrelated diversification typically involves a merger or acquisition between firms that operate in different industries, such as steel and financial services. An alternative to an acquisition strategy is for a firm to create a new business entity from scratch. This decision depends on the outcome of cost-benefit analysis and other top management considerations.

Examples of diversification strategies:

General Electric (GE), Com. - power plan, gas, home alliances, airplane engines.

Apple, Inc. - Apple watches, iPad, AirTag, iPhone, Macintosh.

Amazon. Com, Inc. - streaming video, music, audiobooks, Web Services, grocery.

Samsung, Inc. - Samsung smartphones, tablets, TVs, home appliances, semiconductors, healthcare.

Outsourcing Strategies

As companies strive to improve their operational efficiency, many are turning to outsourcing as a means of achieving this goal. Outsourcing involves partnering with vendors, both domestically and internationally, to obtain necessary inputs or services at a lower cost than producing them in house, while still maintaining high quality standards. Some companies choose to outsource when they do not have the technology, facilities, or expertise needed to produce the desired products or services internally. In recent years, outsourcing strategy has become an increasingly popular strategy for entrepreneurs seeking to optimize their business operations.

Examples of outsourcing strategies:

The following companies are heavily involved in domestic and/or international outsourcing of services, projects, or other inputs:

Alibaba, com.

Dell Technologies, Inc.

McDonald's, Inc.

International Business Machines (IBM), Inc.

Joint Venture Strategies

Numerous firms discover collaborating with other companies, even if they are competitors, to be advantageous. There are several reasons why adopting this strategy is necessary, including:

- Inability to raise sufficient capital, lack of technology, or expertise to undertake a project or establish a business venture independently.

- The opportunity to acquire technical, managerial, marketing, or other skills from the partner.

- The ability to gain business contacts through the partner.

- The ability to expedite the completion of a project or venture.

Joint ventures can lead to friction between partners as a result of cultural differences, disagreements regarding profit distribution, or other business-related issues. To mitigate potential disputes in the future, partners must have a deep understanding of each other and sign a legally binding agreement that outlines the resolution for any potential causes of disagreement.

Examples of joint venture strategies:

Microsoft, Corp., and SAS for building an emergency response system that functions during disasters.

NASCAR and IRACING for speeding to serve fans with a virtual series when sports had to hit the brakes.

Ventec Lie Systems and GM, Inc. for breathing life into rapid-scale manufacturing with much needed ventilators.

Fiserv, Inc. and USDA for enabling grocery stores to accept SNAP electronic payments, right when it mattered.

Defensive Strategies

The prosperity and expansion of businesses depend on a variety of internal and external factors. These factors include economic downturns, natural disasters, conflicts, poor management decisions, and other significant forces. When adversely affected by these factors, companies may opt to take defensive measures such as downsizing their workforce, shutting down certain business units, or even exiting the market entirely due to their inability to sustain operations.

To prevent or reduce the impact of unforeseen internal and external shocks, it is crucial for management to plan the business's future strategies meticulously. This can be achieved through the use of strategic planning methodology, wise decisions, and effective leadership.

Summary

Business strategies are developed to position an enterprise to achieve its desired goals. The choice of strategy is influenced by various factors, such as the enterprise's size, resources, industry, competitive environment, expected return on investment, and top management's risk tolerance. Companies employ various types of strategies, including offensive and defensive approaches, such as differentiation, integration, diversification, outsourcing, and downsizing.

Differentiation strategies are employed to persuade customers that a company's products or services are unique. This can lead to increased profits, market share, competitive advantage, growth, and survival. Integration strategies are used to expand market reach, attain growth, and achieve competitive advantage. Diversification strategies involve expanding the reach of business operations from a single enterprise to a global, multi-business enterprise. Companies pursue outsourcing strategies to attain greater operational efficiency.

As emphasized before, the essence of business strategy is to position a venture in such a way that it can achieve its strategic goals and ultimately, its vision. The end result is realized through a series of managerial decisions and actions. When considered as a whole, the desired end result forms the strategic thrust or business strategy of the venture. An example of a strategy for a hypothetical mini-van manufacturer is the following:

'Our plan is to reach global customers with reliable, long-lasting and well-designed electric mini-vans that are safe to drive, easy to park, and environmentally friendly. The majority of production will be directed towards heavily congested city streets as a convenient mode of transportation.

The strategy can be seen as a broad outline of the company's main thrust to position itself competitively in the marketplace. To execute the strategy, specific financial, operations, and marketing plans and sub-plans must be put in motion for funds, equipment, target production, sells, logistics, quality control, and other aspects of doing business.

Questions

1. What is the differentiation strategy?

2. How would you differentiate an over-the-counter medication from other similar medica-tions sold in supermarkets?

3. Compare diversification strategies to integration strategies.

4. What are the advantages of outsourcing strategies?

Chapter 6

EXECUTING THE STRATEGIC PLAN

"Execution is a specific set of behaviors and techniques that companies need to master in order to have competitive advantage. It's a discipline of its own"

Ram Charan and Larry Bossidy, Execution

Chapter Objectives

- Understand the meaning of strategy execution.

- Describe the requirements of strategy execution.

- Discuss the difference between strategy formulation and execution.

- Illustrate the impact of strategy execution on the venture's competitiveness.

Business strategies are researched, analyzed, and formulated with the purpose of implementation. However, without deployment, strategies are of no use. Strategy implementation refers to a series of managerial decisions and actions aimed at translating strategies into actions throughout the business enterprise. While strategy formulation is the planning phase that involves developing strategic plans for the company, implementation is an action-oriented stage that requires the assembly and deployment of organizational resources to achieve desired results. It is a result-oriented progression that involves the participation of the vast majority of employees.

The Implementation Requirements

According to the Management Essentials course taught by Professor David Garvin at Harvard Business School, effective strategy implementation involves delivering what was planned or promised on time, within budget, at the expected quality level, and with minimal variability – even in the face of unexpected events and contingencies[26].

In a more detailed discussion, successful strategy execution requires entrepreneurs and executives to deploy the necessary inputs to ensure the smooth continuation of this stage of strategic planning. These inputs include:

- Capital budgeting for wages, salaries, raw materials, and other resources.

- Assigning responsibilities among units/departments.

- Instituting AI professional development and other workforce programs.

- Establishing performance control standards and deadlines.

- Forming teams, setting team rules, and selecting team leadership.

- Demonstrating management commitment, support, and follow-up.

- Developing policies and procedures to ensure successful implementation.

- Creating a culture of cooperation, open communication, and teamwork.

- Establishing a system of incentives and rewards for outstanding performance.

- Developing functional strategies (e.g., marketing, finance, logistics, etc.) to facilitate the proper execution of the venture's strategic plan.

---

[26] www.online.hbs.edu.

As mentioned earlier, it is crucial to evaluate the business strategy on two occasions: prior to implementation and after implementation. The same set of general questions discussed in this book earlier can be applied in both situations. The purpose of evaluating the strategy after a period of implementation, such as a year, is to gauge its effectiveness in helping the venture achieve its primary goals and objectives. The assessment outcomes encompass the following:

1. The strategy successfully accomplishes the expected goals and objectives of the venture, indicating that no strategic changes are required.

2. The strategy appears ineffective in attaining the desired goals and objectives. Consequently, corrective actions become necessary. In this scenario, several alternatives should be explored, including (i) reviewing the attainability of the vision, goals, and objectives, taking into account the internal and external environment of the firm, and (ii) assessing the adequacy of resource allocation to execute the strategy. Once the review process is completed, appropriate managerial decisions can be made.

Observing that top management could encounter various obstacles when executing their strategies is crucial. According to Sull et al[27]., executing a strategy involves not only aligning different units within an organization but also coordinating them and adapting to changing market conditions. Managers frequently encounter difficulties relying on their colleagues in other departments or business units, which can result in conflicts and dysfunctional behaviors. Furthermore, while resource allocation is critical, continuous adjustments are necessary to handle unforeseen events. The authors suggest that companies prioritize fostering coordination, building agility, and improving resource allocation to achieve excellent strategy execution.

Performance Measurement

To ensure the effectiveness of strategy implementation, many evaluation criteria can be expressed quantitatively. The choice of the qualitative

---

27 Sull, Donald et al (2015). Why Strategy Execution Unravels – and What to Do About it, *Harvard Business Revies,* 93(3), 57-66.

measures used depends on the nature of the business as well as the goals being measured. Here are some examples of how to measure various organizational performance factors:

Table 1

Performance Measurement Approaches

Goals	Possible Measures
Sales	Units sold; unit price; total revenue, marginal revenue
Output	Number of units; weight of output; size, length of output
Quality	Number of defective units; discoloration; deviation from a standard
Productivity	Revenue divided by total cost; the value of the output divided by the number of hours worked
Customer satisfaction/retention	Survey; interview; number of customer complaints

The actual outcome of a performance target (e.g., goal) is compared to the planned outcome, and any discrepancies are investigated. Necessary actions are then taken to rectify the situation. For instance, if the sales target for a given month was $100,000, but the actual sales were only $80,000, the difference can be investigated to identify the causes of discrepancies.

The Five Ps for Strategy

Given that we have previously explored the process of strategic management (strategic planning) in preceding chapters, it would prove beneficial to acquaint ourselves with Henry Mintzberg's renowned article on strategy[28]. The author presents the notion that strategy can be observed from five distinct perspectives: plan, ploy, pattern, position, and perspective, as detailed below. The author emphasizes that these five Ps embody diverse approaches to defining, formulating, implementing, and evaluating strategy. Furthermore, they can be analytical tools for comprehending an organization's strategic circumstances.

---

28 Mintzberg, Henry (1987). The Strategy Concept I: Five Ps for Strategy, the *California Management Review journal*, 30(1), 11-

Plan: a purposeful course of action or set of guidelines for future decision-making.

Ploy: a specific maneuver or tactic employed to outmaneuver or dissuade competitors.

Pattern: a consistent and coherent behavior or regularity observed over time.

Position: a means of situating an organization or its products within a given environment or market.

Perspective: a shared mindset or worldview that shapes an organization's operational approach.

Summary

Business strategies are formulated with the intention of being put into action. Executing these strategies involves converting them into actionable steps and allocating the required resources. Successful execution entails timely delivery, adherence to budgetary constraints, and meeting predetermined quality standards. It is crucial to assess the effectiveness of the strategy both before its implementation and after its implementation in order to gauge its ability to accomplish key goals and objectives. In cases where the strategy proves to be ineffective, corrective measures become essential, such as reassessing the vision, goals, and objectives, or reallocating resources

Questions

1. Discuss the meaning of strategy execution.

2. Explain the key requirements for strategy execution.

3. Compare and contrast strategy execution and formulation.

4. What are some of the obstacles that could face effective strategy implementation?

PART 2
DIGITAL
TRANSFORMATION

Chapter 7

DIGITAL ENTREPRENEURSHIP

"Think more about what people really want than about what you think they need."

Chris Guillebeau, The $100 startup

Chapter Objectives

- Understand the meaning of digital entrepreneurship.

- Learn the different kinds of digital products.

- Study the steps of establishing a digital products business venture.

- Acquire the knowledge of crafting a business plan.

At the 2022 Digital Economy Meeting held by the Organization for Economic Cooperation and Development (OECD), attendees rallied around the idea that a dependable, environmentally friendly, and equitable digital future is vital for attaining sustained national economic progress. This marks a noteworthy endorsement of AI-driven digital technologies and products, steadily garnering recognition from individuals, businesses, organizations, and nations across the globe. The OECD also underscored the transformative capabilities of the digital economy in bolstering productivity, income levels, and overall societal well-being.

Furthermore, digital entrepreneurship has become increasingly important in recent years due to the rapid expansion of technology and the Internet. This has created numerous opportunities for innovative entrepreneurs to start their own ventures and reap the benefits of growth. Undoubtedly, the emergence of AI invention and innovation has transformed how businesses operate as they adapt to changing technology and consumer demands.

The full force of globalization has made it effortless for digital entrepreneurs to reach international consumers with minimal resources and effort. The internationalization of markets has opened up new avenues and opportunities for entrepreneurs and other firms. Experts predict that the future of digital products is highly promising as entrepreneurs continue to innovate and create products that cater to the changing needs of consumers. Furthermore, with the continued development of AI, virtual reality, blockchain technology, and machine learning, the potential for digital products is expected to expand even further.

Classification of Entrepreneurship?

Entrepreneurship can be broadly categorized into three primary forms: business (commercial), social, and digital. The primary objective of social entrepreneurship is to achieve social objectives by providing goods and services. Social entrepreneurial ventures aim to support society as a whole or specific segments without profit motives.

On the other hand, business and digital entrepreneurial ventures are profit-oriented organizations. Both types share several similar characteristics, including:

- A focus on identifying market opportunities.

- Business entrepreneurs target ordinary goods and services, whereas digital entrepreneurs focus on digital goods and services.

- They also share a willingness to take above-average risks, a focus on growth and profitability, and reliance on venture capitalists, angel investors, or other sources for startup and growth venture funding.

- They utilize advanced means of doing business, such as AI and digital technologies, and deploy business strategies, innovation, and creativity in the management of their firms.

- Finally, visionary entrepreneurs seek both wealth creation and societal benefits.

What is Digital Entrepreneurship?

Digital entrepreneurship is a modern manifestation of the entrepreneurial mindset. It involves individuals who explore, innovate, discover, and ultimately profit from digital commerce. This approach entails the utilization of advanced digital technologies, such as AI, while designing and implementing a business model that caters to the needs of digital customers. The primary focus of this entrepreneurial approach is to create and promote digital goods and services through online transactions to establish a distinct presence in the ever-changing entrepreneurial landscape.

On the other hand, digital technologies "refer to various electronic tools, devices, systems, and resources that generate, store, or process data.[29] "These technologies have become ubiquitous daily, enabling individuals and entrepreneurial firms to create, publish, and market digital content such as images, audio, video, and text.

The Emergence of Digital Entrepreneurship

In recent years, digital entrepreneurship has emerged as a new type of entrepreneurship, joining the ranks of the other two main types: business entrepreneurship and social entrepreneurship. While the primary motivating factors for the rise of each type of entrepreneurship may vary, entrepreneurship itself is a societal necessity because it performs essential functions and roles. Entrepreneurship contributes to innovation, job creation, the introduction of new and improved goods and services, social causes, and economic progress.

The following factors have facilitated the emergence of digital entrepreneurship[30]:

---

[29] What is Digital Technology, https://www.igi-global.com/dictionary/back-basics-electronic-collaboration-education/7723.

[30] See, for example, Qiu, Cai Q. and Man, Mok K. (2021). The Challenges and Solutions for Digital Entrepreneurship Platform in Enhancing Firm's Capabilities, International Journal of Business and Management; 16 (11), 21-25; World Economic Forum (2020). How Digital Entrepreneurs Will Help Shape the World after the Covid-19 Pandem-ic; van Welsum, Desirée (2016). Enabling Digital Entrepreneurs, The World Bank.

- The invention of the internet.

- Advancements in AI technologies.

- The availability of funds for digital entrepreneurship ventures offered by venture capitalists, angel investors, and other investors.

- The attractiveness of many digital products to consumers in terms of price, quality, or functionality.

- The promotional influence of social media networks such as Twitter and Facebook on the demand and use of many digital products.

- The growing utilization of e-commerce and its global reach.

- The ability of digital entrepreneurs to access powerful support technologies such as cloud computing and large data analytics.

- The willingness of digital entrepreneurs to take additional risks to create, identify, and exploit new opportunities with innovative business approaches and models

Digital Products

The realm of digital products is rapidly expanding as technology advances and generative AI gains more interest. With consumers' insatiable desire for new and existing goods and services, the breadth of digital offerings continues to increase remarkably. Table 1 showcases some of the popular digital products that have emerged recently.

Table 1

Example of Digital Products

Coloring pages	Digital art and Photography	Resume templates	Business startup guides
Creative writing Workshops	Consultations	Wallpapers	Proofreading
eBooks	Music	Streaming video services	Selling tickets
Yugo classes	Dance classes	Crafts	Selling posters
Business cards templates	Website themes	Mobile applications	Podcasts
Selling licenses for your digital applications	Nutrition plans	Digital advertising	Online marketplace
Hair and makeup solutions	Online booking	Cryptocurrencies transactions	Digital healthcare tools
Digital security and antivirus software	Webhosting	Cloud-based project management tools	Online banking
Short films	Graphic design tutorials	YouTube banners	illustrations
Repair materials	Creative brief samples	Product comparisons	Set-up tutorials
Astrology or spiritual courses	Digital entrepreneurship Tutorials	Professional editing	Video creation tutorials

The Digital Ecosystem

The digital ecosystem is a complex network of various factors and entities that work together to facilitate the creation, distribution, and consumption of digital content and services. Digital entrepreneurship is a valuable process that brings numerous benefits not only to entrepreneurs themselves but also to society as a whole. It relies on digital technologies to create digital products, both operating within the broader context of the digital ecosystem.

So, what exactly is the digital ecosystem? The Cambridge Dictionary defines an ecosystem as "any complex system of many different people, processes, activities, etc., especially relating to technology, and how they affect each other." The digital ecosystem comprises a vast, interconnected network of digital tools, computers, software, talent, and online activities that work together to enable the creation and sharing of digital products and services across individuals, organizations, government agencies, and the global economy.

The digital ecosystem significantly impacts the development and progress of digital technologies and digital products.

Some of the key entities and factors that comprise the digital ecosystem include:

- Availability of funding.

- Government policies.

- Availability of technical and managerial skills and talents.

- Demand for digital products.

- Cultural attitudes towards technology.

- Entrepreneurial leadership.

- Human and technology networks, innovation centers and incubators.

- Entrepreneurial education.

- National and global economic factors.

What is E-commerce?

E-commerce, an abbreviation for electronic commerce, refers to an online platform for exchanging goods and services. The advancements in computer technology, software development, and internet networks have enabled the creation and widespread use of e-commerce. The primary objective of e-commerce is to facilitate secure domestic and international business transactions. Digital entrepreneurs should understand e-commerce, its role in business growth, its various models, and the security challenges associated with its use. According to estimates, the revenue generated from retail e-commerce will surpass one trillion U.S. dollars by the end of 2023.

Digital entrepreneurs can enjoy numerous benefits from e-commerce, such as lower operational costs, faster transactions, a larger consumer base, customer data collection, transaction scalability regardless of the size or quantity of products transacted, and targeted marketing to reach the desired audience. However, e-commerce also has its drawbacks, including the planning and executing shipping logistics, intense competition, the need to acquire technical skills, and security breach challenges.

The principal categories of e-commerce activities include business-to-consumer (B2C), such as Home Depot selling its products to consumers; consumer-to-business (C2B), such as artists selling their artwork to businesses via online websites; business-to-business (B2B), such as IBM selling supercomputers to Delta Airlines; and business-to-government (B2G), such as Raytheon selling military equipment to the US government.

Additionally, there are government-to-consumer (G2C) activities, such as students paying a late fee to a public library via an official website, and consumer-to-government (C2G) activities, such as individuals paying federal or state taxes via a government website.

Entrepreneurial Career in Digital Products

For several reasons, digital entrepreneurship offers a fascinating career path with limitless potential and opportunities. Firstly, due to economic progress and increased income, digital technologies and applications are rapidly advancing. Secondly, there is a growing demand for innovative, high-quality digital products by many individuals. Thirdly, social media and other communication tools have expanded their reach to promote campaigns for digital and other products. Lastly, the globalization movement intensifies the scope of market opportunities for digital and other products.

Whether digital or otherwise, entrepreneurship is a field of economic activity that requires an entrepreneurial mindset, vision, creativity, and the deployment of winning strategies. The driving force of this field is the pursuit and realization of opportunities. Below are some general guidelines, particularly for aspiring entrepreneurs seeking to establish and grow their digital product business ventures

1. Educate yourself about digital entrepreneurship's nature, risks, monetary costs, efforts, and prospects to ensure that it aligns with your long-term skills and interests.

2. Develop a business concept and model. The concept should provide a statement of the intended line of business, the industry, target customers, and the market. For instance, creating and selling digital athletic shoe images.

3. The business model should focus on the venture's ability to generate profits in the future by calculating the anticipated profitability as the difference between the predicted costs and expected revenue during a given period of time.

4. Explore the market by assessing the potential demand for the product among the target audience (potential customers) to understand how well the product is likely to be received in the market. This initial analysis can be conducted through cost-effective approaches with the help of such tools as ChatGPT, Phind, Google Bard, Microsoft Bing, or by conducting a market survey.

5. Create a vision for the venture, which should inform various constituencies, such as customers, suppliers, and employees, about the venture's long-term target. For instance, becoming the market leader in digital wallpapers.

6. Create a mission statement identifying the venture's business domain and industrial base. An example of a mission statement is developing user-friendly and cost-effective educational software.

7. Determine goals and objectives (specific steps) to achieve those goals. Goals represent desired outcomes or end results, while objectives are concise and short statements of intention. An entrepreneurial venture should have no more than four key goals for implementation, such as increasing sales or improving client satisfaction.

8. Translate goals into objectives to ensure the attainment of desired goals. For instance, to increase sales, specific objectives might include hiring three digital technology staff within the next three months and augmenting the sales budget by an additional $30,000 over the next year.

9. Formulate the business strategy for the venture, which should function as a roadmap that directs entrepreneurs in their decisions and actions, facilitating the realization of the venture's vision and primary objectives. Growth-oriented strategies include differentiation, diversification, and integration. Additionally, generate supplementary strategies for marketing, finance, and other functional areas as required after establishing the venture.

Developing a Business Plan

A business plan is crucial for any venture as it guides future activities and operations. Additionally, it is also necessary when seeking external funding and investments. A well-presented business plan should include the following components:

- A cover page that includes the name and address of the venture, the entrepreneur (s) name (s), and a confidentiality statement.

- An executive summary.

- A statement outlining the venture's value proposition, including the value it will deliver to customers, the problem it seeks to solve, and its product or service features.

- The venture's vision, mission, major goals, and objectives.

- The business model covers cost, revenue, and future profit projections.

- The venture's competitive advantage and what makes it unique.

- A description of the nature of the product (goods/services),

- The target market (local, national, etc.), target customers (e.g., students, women, etc.), economic sector, and industry.

- Channels of distribution.

- Capital, staff, and other resources needed for the venture.

- The organizational structure of the venture and the legal form of the venture (e.g., partnership, corporation, etc.).

Finally, you can develop your business plan with the help of software that provides step-by-step instructions for creating a professionally designed output.

Reaching Customers

Aspiring entrepreneurs must determine the most convenient and cost-effective way to reach potential consumers with their products. Two practical business models are available for small business owners to consider: the e-commerce model and the marketplace model.

The e-commerce model[31] involves creating and maintaining a website for your business. This approach is less expensive than a physical store and allows for targeted marketing to specific market segments. However, there are costs associated with website maintenance and security concerns.

The marketplace model uses a third-party website[32] where the entrepreneur (seller) and the customer conduct transactions. This approach may involve various fees such as listing, advertising, and commission. However, it could provide a reliable and trustworthy platform with a large customer base, lowering marketing costs. Each approach has its own advantages and disadvantages that entrepreneurs must evaluate before making a choice.

---

[31] E-commerce refers to business transactions conducted over the Internet. It involves online buying and selling of goods and services, where money and information exchange occurs through secure communication systems. Nowadays, there are various types of e-commerce, including business-to-consumer (B2C), business-to-business (B2B), government-to-consumer (G2C), and mobile commerce (m-commerce). Examples of web hosting companies in-clude Shopify, GoDaddy, WIX, Squarespace, and Square Online
[32] Examples of such platforms include Amazon, Fiverr, Etsy, eBay, and Big Cartel.

Social Media[33]

Social media has become a powerful tool for connecting people, sharing ideas and hobbies, forming friendships, planning for the future, and achieving various other goals. It has been leveraged by entrepreneurial and other firms such as Robinhood Markets and Peloton Interactive to promote their products and services and achieve success. However, due to legal and other considerations, social media usage should be approached with utmost care and consideration.

So, what exactly is social media? According to Merriam-Webster, social media refers to "forms of electronic communication (such as websites for social networking and microblogging) through which users create online communities to share information, ideas, personal messages, and other content (such as videos)." Entrepreneurs are advised to use social media as a bridge between their firms and potential customers. They should keep in mind the following tips:

- Choose the most suitable social media platform for communication, information dissemination, and advertising.

- Create engaging and informative content to make the site interesting, including the use of short informative videos.

- Learn how to use social media strategically to increase traffic and customer engagement.

- Gather feedback about the impact of your marketing efforts on the target audience.

- Gain insights into customers' purchasing behavior and product preferences.

Critical Success Factors

Digital entrepreneurship, as a specialized branch of entrepreneurship, demands certain critical success factors to steer ventures toward growth

---

[33] In ⁴recent years, social media usage has exponentially increased to encompass billions of individuals worldwide. Among the most prevalent social media platforms are Facebook, YouTube, WhatsApp, Instagram, WeChat, Tik-Tok, Facebook Messenger, Douyin, Telegram, Snapchat, Twitter, LinkedIn, Reddit, Tumblr, Viber, Line, Clubhouse, Twitch, and Discord.

and success. The factors include:

- A clear vision and well-defined goals for the venture.

- Expertise and knowledge of the product and technology.

- Thorough understanding of the industry, target market, and customer preferences.

- Access to sufficient funds and vital skills.

- A product (s) that outshines competitors regarding its features or functionalities.

- Effective strategies, leadership, and teamwork.

Summary

The digital revolution has transformed the world of entrepreneurship, creating new possibilities and challenges for those who dare to innovate and create. In a globalized market, digital entrepreneurs can leverage the power of the Internet to reach customers across borders and niches. They can harness the potential of cutting-edge technology and AI to generate novel and valuable digital goods and services. They can also benefit from the efficiency and convenience of e-commerce, reducing costs and increasing speed.

However, digital entrepreneurs need a clear vision, a solid strategy, and a well-crafted business plan to succeed in this dynamic and competitive environment. They need to understand the digital ecosystem, the complex web of factors and actors that shape the digital economy. They must use social media effectively, to engage and retain their audience. And they need to constantly learn, adapt, and improve, to keep up with the changing demands and opportunities of the digital world

Questions

1. Can you differentiate between digital technologies and digital products? What are the similarities and differences between these two terms?

2. Let's talk about the ecosystem of digital products. What are the

different components and how do they interact with each other?

3. What steps would you take if you were to develop a business plan for a digital products company? What key elements should be included in such a plan?

4. For entrepreneurs in the digital space, what are the critical factors contributing to their success? Can you identify these key success factors?

Chapter 8

Innovation and Artificial Intelligence (AI)

> "If people trust artificial intelligence (AI) to drive a car,
> people will most likely trust AI to do your job"
>
> Dave Waters

Chapter Objectives

- Understand the distinction between invention and innovation.

- Acquire skills for fostering innovation.

- Comprehend the fundamental concepts of AI.

- Familiarize yourself with various types of AI technologies and their applications.

The world of entrepreneurship is widely recognized as a path toward economic progress and overall well-being. It emphasizes the cultivation of an entrepreneurial mindset that values innovation, creativity, and economic potential. Entrepreneurs continuously seek new opportunities to create groundbreaking ventures and introduce improved products and services by leveraging resources and building industries. The advent of AI and its powerful technologies and applications present even more promising prospects for those willing to embrace them. However, this also entails taking on additional risks and dedicating greater efforts to start new businesses or grow existing ones. This marks the era of AI and its dominant influence, especially within the realm of business.

Innovation serves as the driving force behind the development of AI.

The convergence of innovation and AI has revolutionized the global economy, especially in the United States, by providing exceptional technologies, tools, and systems that offer limitless opportunities for individuals with an entrepreneurial mindset and strategic vision. This convergence has also led to a significant expansion of the business landscape, presenting numerous lucrative opportunities for those who are eager to pursue them.

The impact of AI technologies and applications has become increasingly apparent, particularly in late 2022 and early 2023, with the emergence of ChatGPT and other large language models. As innovative entrepreneurial ventures continue to emerge, it is likely that many traditional and inefficient small firms will be phased out in the coming years, similar to what was witnessed during the Industrial Revolution of the 18th century.

What is Innovation? What's Invention?

The Collins dictionary defines innovation as "a new thing or a new method of doing something," whereas the Merriam-Webster dictionary characterizes it as "a new idea, method, or device." Nevertheless, Chesbrough[34] presents a more comprehensive definition of innovation in the business context. He asserts, "Innovation is the creation, development, and implementation of a new product, process, or service, to enhance efficiency, effectiveness, or competitive advantage."

On the other hand, according to the Cambridge dictionary, invention is "something that has never been made before, or the process of creating something that has never been made before." The definitions of invention and innovation demonstrate that they are distinct activities, although they are related. Invention can lead to innovation and vice versa. For example, the invention of the telephone led to the introduction of innovative cellular phones. Invention is the creation of a new product or process for the first time, while improvement on the product or process is viewed as innovation.

---

34 Chesbrough, Henry (2003, p.24). *Open Innovation: The New Imperative for Creating and Profiting from Technology*, Harvard Business Review Press.

Innovation often involves translating invention into reality or practice. The primary purpose of innovation is to add value to goods and services. It can take various forms such as entrepreneurial vision for a unique venture, creative business model, exceptional marketing strategy, and so on. Entrepreneurship involves innovation and the ability to identify rewarding opportunities and seize them before others and act on them.

Table 1 below lists some of the important innovations:

Table 1
Examples of Innovation

Digital Camera	Google Search Engine	Airbnb platform	Lean Startup methodology	Toyota Production System
Online learning platforms	Employee-driven innovation	3D printing of Buildings	Precision farming technology	Design thinking
Telemedicine	Augmented reality shopping	Mobile banking apps	Wearable technology for athletes	Electric vehicles
Plant-based meat alternatives	Self-driving cars	Drone delivery Services	AI-generated music	Virtual reality Experiences
On-demand insurance policies	Digital art platforms	Streaming video Services	Space tourism	Virtual property tours
Online voting	Generative design software	Fitness tracking Devices	Legal chatbots	5G networks
Crowdfunding platforms	Email	GPS	Microchip	Internet

Sources: See for example, Harvard Business School Online, https://online.hbs.edu/blog/post/innovative-product-examples; Satell, Greg (2017). The 4 Types of Innovation and the Problems They Solve, *Harvard Business Revies,* https://hbr.org/2017/06/the-4-types-of-innovation-and-the-problems-they-solve; The Scientist (2021) Top 10 Innovations, https://www.the-scientist.com/features/2021-top-10-innovations-69438; Stone, Daniel (2017). The 10 Inventions that Changed the World, *National Geographic,* https://www.nationalgeographic.com/magazine/article/explore-top-ten-innovations.

Patents and Trademark

The United States Patent and Trademark Office (USPTO)[35] is responsible for registering patents and trademarks for inventors and innovators within the country. There are three major kinds of patents that can be obtained in the United States, as follows:

- Utility Patents include creating a new or improved product, process, or machine. Utility patents are granted for 20 years, giving the owner the exclusive right to use, manufacture, and sell the invention.

- Design Patents - they cover new, original, and ornamental designs for an article of manufacture. Design patents protect the appearance of an object rather than its function and are granted for 15 years.

- Plant Patents are granted to those who have invented or discovered a new and distinct variety of plants, and the patents are valid for 20 years.

The Office utilizes a classification patent method known as the Cooperative Patent Classification (CPC) system, which is also utilized by several European and other nations. This system comprises more than 250,000 subclasses that encompass numerous sectors and industries. The primary patent classes are outlined below:

- Human Necessities.

- Performing Operations; Transporting.

- Chemistry; Metallurgy.

- Textiles; Paper.

- Fixed Constructions.

- Mechanical Engineering; Lighting; Heating; Weapons; Blasting.

- Physics.

---

[35] https://www.uspto.gov/patents-basics/types-patent-applications.

- Electricity.

- Emerging Cross-Sectional Technologies.

Each class of the above categories is divided into subcategories. For example, Human Necessities include patents related to foods and foodstuffs, tobacco, wearing apparel, sports and games, headwear and footwear, furniture and appliances, and so on.

Creativity

As an economic and technological change agent, entrepreneurship requires strategic entrepreneurs to be creative and innovative.[36] These individuals create long-lasting and competitively successful ventures that have a tremendous positive impact on society. Invention, creativity, and innovation are closely related and reinforce each other. An important question to ask is what is creativity, and what are the ways and means for individuals to become more creative?

Encyclopedia Britannica defines creativity as "the ability to create something new, whether it is a new solution to a problem, a new method or device, or a new artistic form," whereas Robert E. Franken, in his book titled Human Motivation, defined creativity as "the tendency to generate or recognize ideas, alternatives, or possibilities that may be useful in solving problems, communicating with others, and entertaining ourselves and others." He highlighted that people are motivated to be creative for the following reasons:

- Need for novel, varied, and complex stimulation.

- Need to communicate ideas and values.

- Need to solve problems.

It is important to recognize that while creativity and innovation are connected, they represent distinct notions. Creativity refers to the act

---

[36] It is believed that innovation, creativity, and imagination are essential skills for success in the modern world and can lead to positive outcomes such as increased productivity, greater job satisfaction, and improved mental health. These skills are also critical for addressing the complex challenges of the 21st century. (Forgeard, M. J. C., and Kaufman, J. C. (2016). Who cares about imagination, creativity, and innovation, and why? A review. *Psychology of Aesthetics, Creativity, and the Arts,* 10(3), 250–269).

of generating fresh ideas, concepts, and possibilities within the mind. On the other hand, innovation encompasses the implementation of those creative ideas in order to address tangible challenges in the real world. In essence, creativity primarily revolves around thinking and idea generation, whereas innovation involves actively taking steps to trans-form those ideas into tangible realities.

Role of Creativity

Creativity plays a crucial role in entrepreneurship and the lives of entrepreneurs. Creative entrepreneurs are capable of:

- Developing a clear business vision and winning strategies.

- Identifying profitable economic opportunities and capitalizing on them.

- Gaining a competitive advantage for their ventures through unique products and services.

- Implementing new technologies and operational methods.

- Creating profitable business models.

- Demonstrating remarkable empathy.

- Communicating effectively with clients, vendors, employees, and other people.

- Solving problems with innovative approaches and methods.

Creativity and AI

The relationship between creativity and AI is inherently direct and strong. This connection is evident in various creative works such as music, art, literature, and construction design. A recent case highlights the relationship between AI and creativity, as a portrait created by a machine learning algorithm was sold at Christie's auction house for $432,500. Additionally, software powered by AI is being employed in music composition to create new pieces of music that seem to have been composed by skilled musicians. In recent years, authors have recommended various techniques and approaches that could greatly help individuals improve the power of their creativ-ity and performance. Table 2 below shows some of the most widely mentioned recommendations:

Table 2

Creativity Enhancement Approaches

Interact and exchange ideas	Engage in creative activities	Learning from experts
Find purpose	Exercise regularly	Learn something new
Develop a wider perspective	Collaborate with Others	Practice writing
Challenge yourself with new opportunities	Keep a Creativity Journal	Set task limits
Overcome a negative attitude or self-criticism	Challenge yourself with new opportunities	Commit yourself to creativity
Allow all ideas to be heard and valued	Look for new sources of inspiration	Reward your curiosity
Consider alternative solutions	Seek out new experiences	Build your confidence
Make time for creative thinking	Take risks to advance your abilities	Visit places
Try new things	Get enough sleep	Read comical books
Change your environment Engage in creative activities	Use your senses	Collaborate with others

Sources: Korstern, Bas (June 17, 2021). Train Your Brain to Be More Creative, *Harvard Business Review,* https://hbr.org/2021/06/train-your-brain-to-be-more-creative; Childs, Peter, et al. (2022). The Creativity Diamond - A Framework to Aid Creativity, *Journal of Intelligence,* 10(4), 73-92; Chris, Olga et al (2022). Training creativity in preschool education, *Astra Sal-vensis,* 2, 191-208; Cherry, Kendra (September 18, 2020). How to Boost Your Creativity: Tips and Strategies, Verywell Mind, https://www.verywellmind.com/how-to-boost-your-creativity-2795046; Indeed, Editorial Team (March 24, 2023). Why Creativity Skills are Important and How to Develop Them, https://uk.indeed.com/career-advice/career-development/creativity-skills.

Causes of Creative Block

Having the ability to think creatively and generate new ideas is an invaluable characteristic that can have numerous benefits in various aspects of life, including personal growth, problem-solving, and professional success. Despite this, many individuals fail to fully utilize their creative potential for several reasons. It is widely acknowledged that creativity is a personality trait that can be developed and nurtured, much like an entrepreneurial mindset or leadership skills. However, some people become so preoccupied with trivial matters in their daily lives that they deliberately or subconsciously prevent themselves from engaging in creative pursuits. Table 3 below lists some of the common internal and external causes that block creativity:

Table 3
Selected Creative Block

Experiencing stress	Being afraid of rejection	Experiencing mental block	Experiencing anxiety
Lack of proactive thinking	Fear of imperfection	Feeling overwhelmed	Being excessively routinized
Fear of the unexpected	Probing too many issues at the same time	Lack of clear direction	Being afraid of failure
Lack of freedom	Organizational disinterest	Insufficient resources	Time pressure
Being unusually serious	Lacking belief in one's Creativity	Avoiding risk-taking	Unpleasant childhood home experience

Sources: See, for example, Tracy, Brian (October 16, 2016). 6 Obstacles to Creative Thinking and How to Overcome Them, *Entre-preneur*https://www.entrepreneur.com/growing-a-business/6-obstacles-to-creative-thinking-and-how-to-overcome-them/282960Tract; HRDQ, What Blocks People from Creativity and Creative Thinking? https://hrdqstore.com/blogs/hrdq-blog/what-blocks-creative-thinking; Wong, Clak-keung S. et al (2003). Barriers to Creativity in the Hotel Industry -- Perspectives of Managers and Supervi-sors, International Journal of Contemporary Hospitality,. Management, 15(1), 29-37.

A Brief History of AI

The history of AI is fascinating and extends over a long period of time preceding the 20th century. This section heavily draws on the Tableau. com article referenced in this book and emphasizes the period of 1950-2023, during which AI has become a field of research and study, in addition to significant developments that have taken place, as indicated below[37]:

[37] Tableau.com, What is the history of artificial intelligence (AI)? https://www.tableau.com/data-insights/ai/history; Simple Lear, What is Artificial Intelligence: Types, History, and Future, https://www.simplilearn.com/tutorials/artificial-intelligence-tutorial/what-is-artificial-intelligence; Press, Jil, 114 Milestones In The History Of Artificial Intelligence (AI), https://www.forbes.com/sites/gilpress/2021/05/19/114-milestones-in-the-history-of-artificial-intelligence-ai/.

In the 1950s, Alan Turing published a paper entitled "Computer Machinery and Intelligence," which suggested a test of machine intelligence called the Imitation Game. A computer scientist named Arthur Samuel developed a program to play checkers, the first to learn the game independently. John McCarthy held a workshop at Dartmouth College on "artificial intelligence" which is the first use of the word, and how it became popular. John McCarthy also created LISP (an acronym for List Processing), the first programming language for AI research. Arthur Samuel created the term "machine learning" in lecturing about teaching machines to play chess better than the humans who programmed them.

In the 1960s, Edward Feigenbaum and Joshua Lederberg created the first "expert system" which was a form of AI program to replicate the thinking and decision-making abilities of human experts. Joseph Weizenbaum created the first "chatterbot" (later shortened to chatbot.

In the 1990s, the Supercomputer 'Deep Blue' was designed, and it defeated the world champion chess player in a match. It was an enormous milestone for IBM to create this large computer.

In the 2000s, Professor Cynthia Breazeal developed the first robot to simulate human emotions with its face. Companies such as Twitter, Facebook, and Netflix started utilizing AI as a part of their advertising and user experience (UX) algorithms. Apple released Siri, the first popular virtual assistant. OpenAI initiated beta testing GPT-3, a model that uses Deep Learning to create code, poetry, and other such language and writing tasks. OpenAI also developed ChatGPT- 4, which became widely utilized, followed by other large language models such as Microsoft Bing and Google Bard.

Table 4

AI-Powered Applications and Uses

Domain	Examples
Productivity and performance Enhancement	Intelligent automation for repetitive and mundane tasks; virtual assistants; project management tools such as Trello.
Customer retention and relations	Chatbots; sentiment analysis tools; customer segmentation tools
Talent acquisition	Ideal an AI-powered talent screening and matching software; Talentsoft, a talent management platform that helps recruiters manage the talent acquisition process.
Sales and marketing	Predictive analytics; marketing automation; customer relationship management (CRM) software
Healthcare	Robotics; Electronic health record systems; wearable devices
Finance	Risk management; portfolio management; fraud detection
Product design	Autodesk Dreamcatcher; SlidWorks simulation; Siemens NX;
Construction design	Building Information Modeling; Generative Design
Property management	Smart building systems; property valuation tools; AI-enabled lease analysis tools
Management	SmartWriter.ai; Computer Vision; Natural Language Processing (NLP).
Education	Intelligent tutoring systems; language learning apps; automated grading systems
Accounting	Tax Planning; Audit Automation; Expense Management
Production	Quality defects deduction; production processes automation; forecasting efficiency losses
Management information systems	Quality Assurance; Service Management; Process Automation
Economics	Economic forecasting; supply chain optimization; pricing optimization
Hunan resources management	Diversity and inclusion; recruitment and selection; workforce planning

Sources: See for example, Chaturvedi, Rijul and Verma, Chaturvedi (2021). Artificial Intelligence-Driven Customer Experience: Overcoming the Challenges, https://cmr.berkeley.edu/2022/03/artificial-intelligence-driven-customer-experience-overcoming-the-challenges/; Pratt, Mary K. (January 24, 2023). 9 top applications of artificial intelligence in business, https://www.techtarget.com/searchenterpriseai/tip/9-top-applications-of-artificial-intelligence-in-business; Davenport, T. H., & Ronanki, R. (2018). Artificial intelligence for the real world. *Harvard Business Review*, 96(1), 108-116; AI Tools for Business: 98 Tools to Skyrocket Your Business (September 9, 2022). https://www.longshot.ai/blog/ai-tools-for-business.

AI Technologies and Applications

Experts point out that the term "AI technologies" is used to indicate the tools and techniques used to create intelligent machines that are intended to simulate human intelligence, such as natural language processing, machine learning, and deep learning. These technologies constitute the building blocks of AI systems that exist today.

On the other hand, AI applications are the practical uses of AI technologies created to solve specific issues or address particular needs. Examples include autonomous vehicles, image recognition software, and chatbots. These applications deploy AI technologies to provide solutions that can automate tasks, improve decision-making, and elevate performance. In other words, AI technologies are the power that enables the creation of AI applications, while AI applications are the end result of the technologies that are designed to solve a variety of problems confronted by society. Some of the major AI-enabled applications are outlined in Table 4 above.

How many AI applications are there? It is very difficult to determine the exact or approximate number of AI applications that have been developed until today (May 2023) due to the numerous ways in which artificial intelligence is being utilized across various economic sectors and industries worldwide. It is certain, however, that AI applications are being developed almost on a daily basis, as the business environment is constantly evolving and the competitive landscape is becoming more complex. Businesses are facing an increasing pace of problems, which further drives the need for developing new AI applications. Moreover, technological applications are conceivable could lead to the creation of other applications.

Table 5

Examples of AI Technologies

Machine Learning	Advanced software algorithms are designed to carry out such tasks as translating languages or answering questions.
Natural Language Processing	It involves teaching machines to understand and interpret human language to enable them to perform such tasks as language translation and text summarization.
Autonomous Vehicles	Self-driving cars that navigate roads with relatively high accuracy.
Cybersecurity	An AI system to identify points of network failure by analyzing network traffic and learning to recognize unusual patterns of activities that might indicate evil intentions.
Speech Recognition	Teaching machines to recognize and interpret human speech with the help of algorithms.
Computer Vision	Deployed with satellite imagery to identify deforestation, illegal logging, and illegal fishing activity.
Brain-Computer Interfaces	This technology is contributing to the development of a brain-controlled a robotic arm that assists a paralyzed person feel again through the human brain interfaces.
Language Modeling:	Language modeling is a process that allows machines to understand and communicate with human beings in a traditional language. OpenAI's GPT-4 illustrates this technology.
Human-machine Collaboration	In several industries, employees increasingly work with or alongside machines that use smart and cognitive functionality to boost human abilities and skills.

Sources: See for example, Mind Majix, Top 10 Artificial Intelligence Technologies, https://mindmajix.com/artificial-intelligence-technologies;Enureka, Top 15 Hot Artificial Intelligence Technologies, https://www.edureka.co/blog/top-15-hot-artificial-intelligence-technologies; Marr, Bernard (September 24, 2021). The 7 Biggest Artificial Intelligence (AI) Trends In 2022;https://www.forbes.com/sites/bernardmarr/2021/09/24/the-7-biggest-artificial-intelligence-ai-trends-in-2022; NIST, Artificial Intelligence, https://www.nist.gov/artificial-intelligence.

AI technologies are numerous and new ones are constantly being invented and innovated. As with AI applications, estimating the number of these technologies is difficult. However, Table 5 above shows some of the most frequently mentioned.

AI Benefits to Entrepreneurs[38]

After briefly exploring some of the most important AI applications and technologies, what are the important benefits that entrepreneurial ventures can derive from the AI revolution? To begin with, the emergence of AI has provided substantial advantages for entrepreneurs by transforming the functioning of their enterprises. One of the most significant benefits of AI is its ability to make superior decisions based on large data sets. By analyzing vast amounts of data in real time, entrepreneurs can make quick and effective decisions that lead to better business outcomes. Data-driven decisions have a greater impact than those based on personal intuition. Data analysis is increasingly being used to identify trends, patterns, and environmental risks.

Another significant benefit of AI is task automation, which enhances productivity and performance. By automating mundane tasks, entrepreneurs can free up time and scarce resources to focus on more critical activities such as market analysis, strategic planning, and innovation. Automation can also lead to more efficient and profitable operations.

AI also enables the implementation of creative business models that make it more efficient to interact with customers. For example, the use of chatbots can significantly engage with customers and provide them with product information and recommendations.

Personalization of goods and services is another advantage of AI. Recent research indicates that AI algorithms can analyze customer behavior and preferences for the enterprise to offer personalized product

---

[38] See, for examples, Lévesque, Moren et al (2022). Pursuing Impactful Entrepreneurship Research Using Artificial Intelligence, Entrepreneur Theory and Practice, 46(4), 803-832 Rios, Luis J (January 13, 2022).3 Entrepreneurial Uses of Artificial Intelligence That Will Change Your Business, Entrepreneur, https://www.entrepreneur.com/science-technology/3-entrepreneurial-uses-of-artificial-intelligence-that-will/403611; Hassan, Abdulsadek et at (2021). The Role of Artificial Intelligencc in Entrepreneurship, https://link.springer.com/chapter/10.1007/978-3-030-93464-4_52.

recommendations, leading to increased customer satisfaction, loyalty, and business growth.

To sum up, AI has the potential to revolutionize the way businesses operate by providing insights derived from large data sets, automation, and the adoption of innovative business models. The advantages of AI outweigh the potential drawbacks, such as the elimination of low-skilled jobs and the potential disappearance of many inefficient small firms. Entrepreneurs who embrace AI can gain a significant competitive advantage and position their ventures for success in a highly competitive business landscape.

AI technologies and applications offer power, flexibility, and diversity that can help companies grow and thrive. Companies can leverage AI to achieve their growth-oriented goals by adopting strategies such as differentiation and diversification.

To fully capitalize on these benefits, entrepreneurs should develop business strategies incorporating appropriate software and effectively leverage AI and human skills.

A Path to Innovation

Let's first summarize the types of innovation in business firms. The Organization for Economic Cooperation and Development (OECD) has introduced a comprehensive model for classifying innovation into four categories[39]:

- Product innovation involves introducing new or improved products, as well as adding new features or functionalities to existing products. Examples of product innovation include color television, smartphones, and self-driving automobiles.

- Process innovation refers to the development of new or improved methods of production or service delivery. Examples of process innovation include Just-In-Time-Inventory and the use of robots in manufacturing.

---

39 The Organization for Economic Cooperation and Development, https://www.oecd.org/innovation/inno/types-of-innovation.htm.

- Marketing innovation involves adapting new marketing and sales strategies, improving channels of distribution, and deploying social media to attract and retain clients.

- Organizational development includes a variety of activities aimed at improving the effectiveness of the organization and enhancing its chances of survival and growth. Examples of organizational development include adapting new business models, organizational structures, and managerial systems and policies.

Product innovation can occur either gradually over time or suddenly through a breakthrough. Additionally, another type of innovation that is often discussed in published research is disruptive innovation. This type of innovation involves the creation of a new market by a business enterprise, the development of a new business model, or the introduction of a modified product that creates a new market.

In recent years, many organizations, particularly mid-sized and large business firms, have turned to AI technologies and applications to assist in their innovation efforts.

As indicated earlier, the rapid advancement of AI technologies has opened up a wide spectrum of AI applications, creating numerous business opportunities for entrepreneurs and others in recent years. To take advantage of these opportunities, several requirements must be met, including the following:

- Assess your skills, experience, and qualifications for entrepreneurial activity. This includes mindset, creative thinking, funds, and hard work.

- Create a clear vision for your business venture, including its business domain, business model, product, and target customers.

- Understand the environment surrounding your target market, such as the intensity of competition, consumer demand, product price structure, and product utility.

- Realize how your intended product is planned to be different from existing products (if any) and what additional utility it provides to incentivize potential customers to purchase it. In other words, what's special about your product?

- Master the field of business strategies to become a strategic entrepreneur.

- Learn about AI applications (and technologies) that are essential for your industry and the intended venture.

- Select the applications (or technologies) related to your planned venture.

- Study the market at the beginning and develop a business plan with the help of business planning software.

Entrepreneurship involves the crucial task of identifying and evaluating potential opportunities and subsequently capitalizing on the most promising ones. As AI technologies and applications continue to gain momentum, the global economy, including that of the United States, presents many lucrative opportunities that strategic entrepreneurs must proactively explore, analyze, and leverage.

Table 6 highlights some of the AI-related business prospects that industry experts and others have recently discussed:

Table 6

AI-Powered Business Opportunities

Natural language processing & text analysis	Metaverse marketing	Virtual assistants	Automated customer service
Video generator	Augmented reality-based jewelry store app business	Customer support business	e-learning apps business
Data management	Auto-generating report	Retail business	Subscription-based delivery app
Roadside car accident app	Photo editing app	Skin analysis tool	Marketing agency
Content creation business	Medical equipment business	Online poker playing business	Management consultant
Recruitment agency	Build software for different applications such as advertising, logo making, etc.	Language Translation	Crop pricing
Livestock tracking	healthcare startups	Architectural design	Crop disease detection
Name generator tool	Farm management	Hair analysis	Wealth Builder
Butler business app	Tax written service	Recommendation engine	Storytelling app

Sources: see for example, KR, Rajalekshmy (February 14, 2023). 9 Promising Artificial Intelligence Startup Ideas For 2023, https://www.aiplusinfo.com/blog/9-promising-artificial-intelligence-startup-ideas-for-2023/; Walls, Pat (August 31, 2022). 40 AI Based Business & Startup Ideas (2023), https://www.starterstory.com/ai-business-ideas; AI Business Ideas for Startups and Entre-preneurs (February 1st 2023). https://hackernoon.com/ai-business-ideas-for-startups-and-entrepreneurs; 7 Innovative Business Ideas Using AI and ChatGPT to Make Money, https://bootcamp.uxdesign.cc/7-innovative-business-ideas-using-ai-and-chatgpt-to-make-money-20ba1c93f115

Summary

Entrepreneurs have a remarkable opportunity to leverage the potential of AI in order to enhance their business ventures and surpass competitors. The applications of AI in the business realm are rapidly expanding. By integrating AI technologies and applications, entrepreneurial ventures can enhance their operational efficiency and achieve cost savings. AI enables businesses to streamline their operations, resulting in improved productivity.

AI can provide profound insights into market trends and economic patterns. This empowers businesses to make well-informed decisions and take proactive measures to maintain competitiveness. Moreover, AI aids entrepreneurs in their innovation endeavors, facilitating the creation of new products and services. By employing AI-powered cybersecurity technology, entrepreneurial firms can safeguard themselves against attacks and ransom threats. Ultimately, AI equips firms with the means to attain greater success and profitability.

Lastly, as AI technologies and applications continue to progress and become more accessible, entrepreneurs who embrace this trend and harness its advantages are better positioned to thrive in today's fiercely competitive business environment.

Questions

1. Explain the meaning of innovation.

2. What are some of the causes of innovation block?

3. Discuss the difference between AI technologies and AI Applications.

4. Elaborate on some of the entrepreneurial opportunities in the AI field.

Chapter 9

THE ENTREPRENEURIAL MINDSET

> "Being an entrepreneur is a mindset.
> You have to see things as opportunities all the time"
>
> Epic marketing Consultants

Chapter Objectives:

- Understand the concept of mindset.

- Recognize the importance of an entrepreneurial mindset.

- Differentiate between a growth mindset and a fixed mindset.

- Gain familiarity with factors that influence a growth mindset.

Entrepreneurial mindset and opportunity recognition are closely related concepts that have been intertwined throughout modern history. Entrepreneurs have been business leaders in free market societies for centuries, driving innovation and economic progress. These strategic thinkers possess the vision and skills necessary to create new ventures and generate employment opportunities. Over time, successful entrepreneurs become strategic entrepreneurs who leave a lasting impact on society and the world.

Entrepreneurs and Strategic Entrepreneurs

A distinction needs to be made between the concepts of entrepreneurs and strategic entrepreneurs. Although both types of individuals share characteristics such as being innovators, visionaries, and seekers of opportunities, strategic entrepreneurs are highly accomplished individuals, many of whom are serial entrepreneurs, influential, and widely known. This is in contrast to nascent or burgeoning entrepreneurs.

For example, the United States has witnessed numerous strategic entrepreneurs in recent years such as Bill Gates (co-founder of Microsoft Corp), Steve Jobs (co-founder of Apple Inc.), Elon Musk (founder of Tesla, Space X, and owner of Twitter), Jeff Bezos (founder of Amazon. com), and Mark Zuckerberg (co-founder of Facebook).

An ordinary entrepreneur is different from a small business owner in the following respects:

- The entrepreneur's business geographic horizon is not limited to a locality, state, or country. The vision is global.

- The entrepreneur is risk-taking above and beyond an ordinary individual.

- The entrepreneur's mindset is about innovation and opportunity seeking.

On the other hand, small business owners generally possess the following characteristics:

- They own a business that provides goods and/or services tailored to a specific locality, such as mom-and-pop shops, taxi drivers, and lawyers' offices.

- They are risk-averse and have limited capital, managerial skills, and technical abilities.

- They generate only a limited number of employment opportunities.

- They typically lack the inclination or motivation for innovation or change.

- They operate in an intensely competitive market environment like the food industry.

The Mindset

As per the Merriam-Webster dictionary, "mindset" encompasses two meanings: (1) a mental attitude or inclination and (2) a fixed state of mind. The Britannica dictionary defines the "brain" as the organ located in the head responsible for controlling functions, movements, sensations, and thoughts. Studies suggest that the brain and the mind are distinct concepts, yet intricately connected and intertwined. While the brain is a tangible entity, the mind encompasses an amalgamation of thoughts, perceptions, beliefs, and attitudes.

In addition, findings about the mind and brain[40] reveal the following: (a) the mind contains billions of brain cells, (b) most people don't use 10 percent of brain capacity, (c) information travels to and from the brain at 250 miles per hour, (d) memories can change over time, and (e) the brain requires a constant supply of oxygen.

Daskal[41] identified seven types of mindsets that the author recommends individuals practice and gradually grow, as indicated below:

1. Self-trust mindset.

2. Goal-setting mindset.

3. Patient mindset.

4. Courageous mindset.

5. Focused mindset.

6. Positive mindset.

7. Learning mindset.

Fixed Mindset and Growth Mindset

A distinction is made between a growth mindset and a fixed mindset. A growth mindset, as compared to a fixed mindset, is the mindset

---

[40] Blackham, Allice, 10 Interesting Facts About the Human Mind That You May Not Know, https://selecthealth.org/blog/2021/06/interesting-facts-about-the-human-mind, uploaded in March 2023.

[41] Daskal, Lolly (July 17, 2015). 7 Mindsets That Will Radically Improve Your Life Right Now, Inc.

of an individual who constantly seeks to learn, grow, and succeed. It is the mindset of achievers who tirelessly explore ways and means to simplify their lives and tasks and get things done better. Popular terms used to convey the meaning of mindset include outlook, attitude, and mentality. Moreover, it is suggested[42] that Individuals with a growth mindset believe that learning can bring about change in a person.

On the other hand, those who have a fixed mindset do not believe in the possibility of change and tend to emphasize their innate abilities and competence. As a result, they tend to avoid challenges that could potentially make them look incompetent or unintelligent. Essentially, people with a fixed mindset are less resilient when faced with performance failures because they view putting in more effort as a confirmation of their lack of ability.

When discussing lifelong learning, which refers to the process of embracing learning throughout one's life, it is pointed out[43] that there are two perspectives to consider: the system-level perspective and the individual-level perspective. It's pointed out that a lifelong learning mindset typically involves three common features: (1) epistemic curiosity, (2) strategic thinking, and (3) resilience. Epistemic curiosity is a drive to learn new things, strategic thinking is a mode of processing new information that emphasizes the big picture, and resilience involves directing resources to overcome challenges when learning something new. These three features represent a set of beliefs, attitudes, and tendencies displayed by lifelong learners, and these concepts play a crucial role in the learning process and outcomes related to the individual's work performance and success.

According to experts, individuals with a fixed mindset tend to express their feelings in various ways, such as[44]:

- Giving up easily by saying "This is too difficult, so I might as well

---

[42] Kouzes, Tae K. and Posner, Barry Z. (2019), Influence of Managers' Mindset on *Leadership Behavior, Leadership and Organization Development Journal*, 40(8), 829-844.

[43] Drewery et al. (2020). Lifelong Learning Mindset and Career Success: Evidence from the Field of Accounting and Finance, *Higher Education, Skills and Work–Based Learning*, 10(3), 567-580.

[44] 8 fixed Mandate and Growth Mindset Examples and How to help Improve, https://selfsufficientkids.com/growth-mindset-examples-and-fixed-mindset-examples/

give up."

- Belittling their own abilities by saying "I'm not as good as others, so why bother trying?"

- Avoiding challenges at any cost to avoid looking foolish.

- Taking feedback personally instead of using it constructively.

- Stopping their efforts to improve once they find a task easy, fearing failure if they push themselves further.

- Feeling discouraged by comparing themselves to others and concluding that they're not as good, so why try?

- Defining success solely by the end result.

- Assuming they already know everything there is to know.

The Entrepreneurial Mindset

Entrepreneurial mindset refers to a mental state that transforms an individual into an entrepreneur by enabling them to analyze the world and identify the opportunities and possibilities it presents. Essentially, it is one's mentality that allows one to embrace the entrepreneurial spirit and embark on the path of entrepreneurship.[45]

Education researchers have been studying mindset theory, which refers to how individuals perceive themselves, or self-theory. The focus is on fixed versus growth mindsets. People with a fixed mindset believe intelligence is predetermined and cannot be improved, while those with a growth mindset believe intelligence can be developed. For instance, the strongest predictors of student success are persistence, fortitude, resilience, and effort. Therefore, there are two contrasting beliefs about intelligence: innate and unchangeable, or developmental and malleable. This second belief is called incremental theory, and those who subscribe to it believe intelligence can grow over time[46].

---

[45] Kouakou, Konan K. E. et al (2019). Evolution View of Entrepreneurial Mindset Theory, *International Journal of Business and Social Science,* 10 (6), 116-120.
[46] Nestor, Asley, L. (2017). Investigation Mindset Theories: The Implications for Classroom Instruction and Profes-sional Development, Ph.D. dissertation, School of Education, University of Pittsburgh.

The entrepreneurial mindset is a key concept in the field of entrepreneurship, which authors have examined from various perspectives, and offered several informative definitions, as follows:

- "The ability to recognize and create opportunities, take calculated risks, and persist in the face of failure."[47]

- "A set of beliefs, thought processes, and ways of viewing the world that drive entrepreneurial behavior, including creativity, problem-solving skills, and a propensity for innovation."[48]

- "A combination of traits and behaviors that enable individuals to identify and pursue opportunities, adapt to changing circumstances, and create value for themselves and others"[49]

- "Attitudes, skills, and behaviors that enable individuals to identify opportunities, overcome challenges, and create value in various settings."[50]

- "Attitudes, skills, and behaviors that enable individuals to identify opportunities, overcome challenges, and create value in various settings."[51]

It's also asserted that the entrepreneurial mindset is a way of thinking that involves four key components: (1) opportunity recognition, (2) risk-taking, (3) innovation, and (4) proactiveness.[52]

On the basis of these and many other definitions, the key ingredients of the entrepreneurial mindset are the individual's ability, beliefs, behavior,

---

[47] Hennessey, M. G. (2017). Entrepreneurial mindset: The key to becoming a successful entrepreneur. *Journal of En-trepreneurship Education*, 20(2), 51-54.

[48] *Cornwall, J. (2017). The Entrepreneurial Mindset. In M. Brännback & A. Carsrud (Eds.), Revisiting the Entre-preneurial Mind: Inside the Black Box: An Expanded Edition (pp. 15-28). Springer International Publishing. https://doi.org/10.1007/978-3-319-59954-5_2*

[49] Eckhardt, J. T., & Shane, S. A. (2013). The individual-opportunity nexus. In Handbook of research on entrepreneurship and creativity (pp. 3-24). Edward Elgar Publishing.

[50] Global Entrepreneurship Monitor (GEM) (2020, p. 21) Global Entrepreneurship Monitor 2019/2020 Global Report. London Business School.

[51] Global Entrepreneurship Monitor (GEM). (2020, p. 21). Global Entrepreneurship Monitor 2019/2020 Global Report. London Business School.

[52] Daspit, Joshua et al (2023). Entrepreneurial mindset: An integrated definition, a review of current insights, and direc-tions for future research, *Journal of Small Business Management*, 61(1), 1-19.

attitude, and skills to identify and capture economic opportunities. Experts suggest using various methods to power one's personality traits such as intelligence, talent, and performance. These various approaches can assist individuals in developing a growth mindset and moving away from a fixed mindset. Table 1 below lists the most widely mentioned suggestions to improve growth mindset:

Table 1

Suggestions to Improve Growth Mindset

Learn from criticism instead of getting defensive or upset.	Pay attention to your words and thoughts.
Emphasize the process over the outcome.	Practice self-reflection
Practice self-compassion.	Embrace challenges as opportunities
Be aware of your fixed mindset.	View failure as a learning opportunity.
Try different tactics to coach yourself in exploring new paths.	Take a step deeper into authenticity
Focus on effort, not talent	Acknowledge and embrace imperfection in yourself
Own your mind	Stop seeking approval from others
Be realistic	View challenges as opportunities
Take risks in the company of others	Practice will lead to improvement and self-development
Acknowledge your weaknesses; work to improve them	"Not yet" is okay. When struggling with a task.
Redefine "genius" Everyone has strengths.	Cultivate resilience. Persist and opportunities will come.

Sources: News Stanford Education; Psychologytoday.com; Opecncolleges.edu.au. Uploaded in March 2023; From Fixed Mindset to Growth Mindset: The Complete Guide, https:// nesslabs. com/growth-mindset.

Summary

Experts have identified two theories related to mindset: the incremental theory and the entity theory. The incremental theory, also known as the growth mindset, proposes that an individual's skills and abilities can be improved through effort and persistence. On the other hand, the entity theory, also known as the fixed mindset, maintains that an individual's skills and abilities are predetermined and may change only slightly.

The entrepreneurial mindset is a critical aspect of taking on new projects, leading innovation, and assuming leadership roles. It reflects an individual's approach and thinking, indicating their ability to achieve goals, adapt to changes, and focus on tasks. Research has demonstrated that possessing an entrepreneurial mindset positively affects leadership and business performance. It also indicates that an individual's mindset can impact others in an organizational context, especially concerning work engagement, teamwork, productivity, and corporate citizenship.

Moreover, entrepreneurial mindset is what drives entrepreneurs to perceive, decide, and act in various ways, including:

- Developing a vision and setting goals.

- Creating strategies for success and excellence.

- Pursuing innovation.

- Identifying, creating, and seizing opportunities.

- Establishing ventures and creating value.

Questions

1. Can you clarify the distinctions between fixed and growth mindsets?

2. Could you offer some illustrations of a fixed mindset?

3. What are the critical components of an entrepreneurial mindset?

4. As a consultant, what steps would you take to cultivate a growth mindset among a group of employees within a business enterprise?

Chapter 10

DIGITAL MARKETING

"It's hard to find things that won't sell online"
Jeff Bezos

Chapter Objectives

- Learn the differences between traditional marketing and digital marketing.

- Recognize the attributes of digital marketing.

- Understand the pillars of digital marketing.

- Identify key elements of content marketing.

A company or business entity typically carries out four fundamental functions. Firstly, it provides valuable products or services to its customers. Secondly, it handles its finances and operations. Thirdly, it promotes its offerings to potential customers. Lastly, it oversees and manages its workforce and other resources. To ensure the smooth functioning of the organization, the entrepreneur or business owner must engage in strategic planning, efficient organization of business operations, appropriate allocation of resources, and effective leadership and supervision of employees. Moreover, the entrepreneur is responsible for identifying and capitalizing on business opportunities to steer the venture toward sustainable success and growth.

What is Marketing?

Marketing is defined by the American Marketing Association (AMA) as "the activity, set of institutions, and processes for creating, communicating, delivering, and exchanging offerings that have value for customers, clients, and society at large." This definition includes three key components:

1. Activities, processes, and organizations that primarily offer goods and services;

2. Activities, processes, and organizations that communicate, exchange, and deliver goods and services; and

3. The spectrum of activities, processes, and organizations add value to the population.

Whether traditional or digital, marketing is fundamental in facilitating a company's growth and competitive advantage. It encompasses various organizational functions, such as identifying and retaining potential customers, advertising, and promotion, selling goods and/or services to target customers, delivering output in the target market, strengthening the company's market position, and developing and implementing strategies to achieve its objectives.

The marketing department, in collaboration with other units, is responsible for offering customers differentiated output that captures their interest and generates demand. Traditional marketing follows a grand strategy based on four pillars, known as the 4 Ps. These pillars are:

1. Product: Design and create goods and/or services that meet the needs or desires of the intended target customers.

2. Price: Ensure that the price of the output reaching customers is competitive for comparable goods or services offered in the target market. Overpriced output could be pushed out of the marketplace.

3. Place: Choose the necessary platforms or outlets, online or otherwise, to make it convenient for customers to purchase your output.

4. Promotion: Utilize various communication channels to promote, sell, and increase customer loyalty.

On the other hand, the AMA defines digital marketing as "the use of digital or social channels to promote a brand or reach consumers. This type of marketing can be executed on the Internet, social media, search engines, mobile devices, and other channels. It requires new ways of marketing to consumers and understanding the impact of their behavior". The definition of digital marketing implies that this mode of marketing is a subset or branch of traditional marketing that has been practiced worldwide for centuries. The definition also indicates the following features of digital marketing:

1. This activity is performed online, using digital tools.

2. Computers and specialized software facilitate it.

3. It is carried out via several communication channels or platforms, including social media and search engines.

4. Its focus is on increasing brand awareness of goods and services.

5. Its deployment requires the utilization of certain strategies, in addition to gaining insight into the purchasing behavior of customers.

The Importance of Digital Marketing

- Digital marketing contributes to increased output, investment, employment, and national income, just like traditional marketing. It also serves as an engine for innovation and the creation of new business ventures, industries, and economic sectors.

- Digital marketing is an effective means of information sharing and communication with customers.

- It is more cost-effective to deploy than other means and has global reach.

- It can target specific customers or groups of customers.

- It can be designed to generate customer feedback.

- It provides a convenient approach to shopping and payment.

- It is the fastest means for commercial transactions.

- With proper software safeguards, it is the most secure method of commercial transactions.

- It facilitates the expansion of trade (exports and imports of goods and services) among nations.

Essentials of Digital Marketing[53]

In recent years, the explosive expansion of digital marketing and its far-reaching global influence can be attributed to a number of crucial components that form its foundation and garner widespread consumer adoption. It is highly advisable for entrepreneurial enterprises to fully grasp these essential of digital marketing in order to achieve success and gain a sustainable competitive edge, as discussed below:

Content marketing

Marketing is a crucial function of any business enterprise, as it ensures that there is continuous and growing demand for the enterprise's goods and/or services. Typically, the marketing responsibility is assigned to the marketing department or division. However, with the advent of AI, digital applications, sophisticated data analytics, and Chat GPT, many traditional marketing activities have transformed into digital marketing, with an expanding scope of functions that primarily include digital communication with customers via such platforms as social media, email marketing, blogs, and videos.

The functionality of digital marketing involves several pillars (or components), including content marketing. The term *content* refers to the message, information, or data contained in the marketing communication directed towards a specific customer or group of customers. In designing, writing, and delivering content marketing, the

---

[53] See, for example, Kannan, P. K. and Li, Hongshuang Alice (2017). Digital Marketing: A framework, Review and Research Agenda, *International Journal of Research in Marketing,* 34(1), 22-45; Kee, Angel Wong An and Yazdanifard, Rashad (2015). The Review of Content Marketing as a New Trend in Marketing Practices, *International Journal of Management, Accounting, and Economics,* 2(9), 1055-1064.

following guidelines should be observed to convey the exact message to the target audience, and ensure the realization of maximum benefits for the enterprise:

- Learn about the needs, desires, and interests of your target customers for your goods and/or services.

- Define the goal for your content marketing to align with the enterprise's strategic goals.

- Formulate your marketing message to resonate with your target customers.

- Deliver your message via a desired digital platform, such as social media, blogs, emails, or other channels, to reach the largest segment of your target audience.

- Strive for clarity, simplicity, and conciseness in your writing to achieve meaningful customer engagement. Whenever possible, include visual displays to enhance the effectiveness of your message.

- Utilize appropriate software or platform services to generate feedback about website traffic and digital marketing efforts.

Social media marketing

Social media is an extensive network of websites, people, and technology applications that has become an essential medium of communication and information exchange among billions of people and business firms worldwide. It has also emerged as a cost-effective marketing outlet for budding entrepreneurs and small business owners. With proper strategic initiative, marketers can derive huge benefits from the utilization of social media, as summarized below:

- Establishing contacts and strengthening relations with potential customers.

- Learning about consumer demand and behavior in specific regions or countries for goods or services offered by your firm.

- Promoting brand awareness.

- Forming a competitive position in the marketplace and stimulating demand for the firm.

- Gaining publicity and the possibility to enhance the firm's reputation.

- Generating leads that could increase website traffic.

- Helping to conduct market research and analysis.

- Absence of barriers to entry.

Email marketing

Email marketing is a vital means of customer communication to build relationships, promote brand awareness, develop loyalty, and increase the firm's revenue. To be an effective and reliable channel for customer relations, emails should be designed and delivered in a timely manner, with the intention of observing standard rules of business etiquette, accuracy, and respect.

There are several specialized email marketing software templates available in the market that facilitate customized email campaigns. Utilizing these templates can improve the market position of entrepreneurial firms. However, email writing experts recommend some excellent guidelines for writing effective email marketing campaigns. For instance, Geoffrey James of Inc magazine (http://www.inc.com/Geoffrey-james/) has offered a few guidelines, including the following:

- Send emails during off-hours.

- Use a short, relevant subject line.

- Address the recipient by their first name.

- Showcase the uniqueness of your goods/services.

- Pack a benefit into the first 20 words.

- Avoid unfamiliar acronyms and buzzwords, and be precise.

- Ask a yes/no question.

- Never assign homework.

- Measure your results.

Moreover, Luisa Zhou (March 7, 2023) published an online article entitled Email Marketing ROI Statistics: The Ultimate List in 2023 (www.luisazhou.com) in which the following interesting statistics are revealed:

1. Email marketing generates $42 for every $1 spent.

2. Mobile devices account for about 60 percent of email opens.

3. 64 percent of small businesses use email marketing.

4. 99 percent of email users are checking their email daily.

5. There are 4.3 billion people worldwide with email addresses.

Mobile marketing

With the advent of smartphones and the rapid advancement of digital technologies, marketers have increasingly begun to deploy mobile marketing as a powerful tool for communicating with customers. Mobile marketing uses SMS (short message service), which is a brief personal text message delivered via electronic devices such as smartphones, tablets, smartwatches, and other communication mediums. Mobile marketing can also take many forms, including quick response (QR) codes.

No matter what form of mobile marketing is used, it can benefit businesses in several ways:

- It is a convenient and economical means of communicating with customers.

- It provides relevant, condensed, and timely information to recipients.

- It acts as a promotional tool for goods and services.

- It allows customers to communicate back to senders easily.

- Its effectiveness can be measured by providing feedback on return on investment (ROI).

- It is an essential component of an overall digital marketing strategy.

Advertising

Advertising serves as a window into the soul of a business, representing the initial impression customers have of a company and potentially determining whether a sale is made or lost. In many ways, it is skin to a gourmet meal crafted by a top-notch restaurant. Like a meal, advertising should exude a sense of warmth and hospitality while also possessing a unique flair that sets it apart from the competition.

The ingredients of an advertisement should be of the highest quality and meticulously chosen to create a memorable and satisfying sensory experience. Much like a skilled chef who takes pride in their creations, marketers should also take pride in the messages they convey to the world, delivering them with respect to all those seeking what they have to offer.

Advertising takes various forms, but digital channels like social media have been the most prominent in recent years. Other significant channels include television, radio, magazines, and billboards. According to the official Australian government website (https://business.gov.au), advertising provides the following advantages:

- Expands the customer base of the business.

- Enhances customer awareness of the brand and enterprise.

- Highlights the benefits of the goods and services offered.

- Communicates essential information about the bus

- Provides a competitive edge over rivals.

Finally, Advertising not only introduces new products and services to customers but also helps businesses expand their market reach and increase their revenue streams.

Summary

Digital marketing is revolutionizing traditional marketing by altering how businesses engage with customers. It impacts how consumers discover and explore products and services, how marketers approach them, how they make purchases and payments, and how their purchasing habits are analyzed.

The overarching aim of any marketing strategy is to offer customers the most satisfying experience possible, ensuring they remain devoted and continue supporting the business. In digital marketing, this objective is achieved through fundamental activities known as the essentials of digital marketing, including content marketing, social media marketing, email marketing, mobile marketing, and advertising.

As technology continues to advance, digital marketing is becoming increasingly prominent within the field of marketing due to its undeniable impact on brand loyalty and sales growth for businesses. According to statistical data published by Demand Sage (https://www.demandsage.com), digital advertising spending is projected to reach $602 billion by 2023. The data also reveals that Facebook and Google offer the highest return on investment and that smartphones are responsible for 55 percent of the world's internet traffic. The data also show that 72 percent of the marketing budget goes toward digital marketing.

Questions

1. Describe the role of marketing in a business and its objectives.

2. Explain the characteristics and advantages of digital marketing.

3. Analyze the key components and guidelines of content marketing.

4. Identify the advantages of advertising for entrepreneurial businesses.

Chapter 11

SELF-LEADERSHIP

"Mastering others is strengths, mastering oneself is true power"
Lao Tsu

Chapter Objectives

*   Understand the concept of self-leadership.

*   Recognize the relationship between self-leadership and entrepreneurship.

*   Learn the theoretical aspects associated with self-leadership.

*   Identify the skills required to master self-leadership.

Self-leadership is a crucial aspect of one's personality as it involves reflecting on oneself, assessing strengths and weaknesses, exercising self-control, and navigating human interactions effectively. Higher levels of self-leadership are associated with a greater probability of individual success. Numerous scholarly studies have shown that self-leadership is closely intertwined with entrepreneurship and serves as a reliable predictor of an individual's ability to manage themselves successfully and have a positive impact on those around them.

Attaining self-leadership requires dedication to learning its essential ingredients and methodically planning to master them. Self-leadership is, indeed, a skill that digital and other entrepreneurs need to acquire, develop, and utilize to guide their teams and business ventures toward sustaina-ble growth and market dominance.

What is Self-leadership?

Self-leadership is viewed as the process by which individuals control their own actions, influencing and leading themselves through the use of specific sets of behavioral patterns. This includes self-imposed strategies for managing performance, as well as self-influence that capitalizes on motivational values.[54]

There are several sources of self-leadership, which include: (1) self-awareness (knowing one's strengths, weaknesses, and values), (2) self-motivation (the ability to lead one's actions towards achieving desired goals), (3) self-discipline (controlling one's urges and sticking to a plan), (4) self-confidence (belief in one's abilities), and (5) self-control (the ability to regulate one's emo-tions and responses).

Over the past few decades, scholars have examined the theoretical aspects of self-leadership from various perspectives, which are summarized below[55]:

- Self-leadership is a systematic approach that involves a set of actions and mental strategies to lead individuals toward higher levels of performance and effectiveness.

- Its main components include the pursuit of virtue, collaboration, and emotional intelligence, and it expands on self-management, which is rooted in self-control theory.

- It involves observing and managing oneself, while leadership is about how individuals influence others.

- Self-leadership demands personal qualities such as self-discipline,

---

[54] Neck, Christopher P. and Houghton, Jeffery D. (2006), "Two decades of self-leadership theory and research: past developments, present trends, and future possibilities", Journal of Managerial Psychology, Vol. 21 No. 4, pp. 270-295; Manz, Charles C. (1986), "Self-leadership: toward an expanded theory of self-influence processes in organizations", Academy of Management Review, 11 (4), 585-600.

[55] See, for example, Gesell, Izzy (2007). Am I Talking to Me? The Power of Internal Dialogue to Help or Hinder Our Success, *Journal of Quality and Participation,* 30(2), 20-21; Godwin, Jeffrey L. et al (1999). The impact of thought self-leadership on individual goal performance A cognitive perspective, *Journal of Management Development,* 18(2), 153-170; Markham, Steven E. and Markham, Ian S. (1995). Self-management and self-leadership reexamined: A levels-of-analysis perspective, *Leadership Quarterly,* 6(3), 343-359.

self-knowledge, self-honesty, and self-awareness.

- The strategies associated with self-leadership include (a) behavior-focused strategies, (b) natural reward strategies, and (c) constructive thought strategies.

- Self-leadership is crucial to employees' enthusiasm for commitment and performance, thus empowering organizations.

- Self-talk is at the heart of self-leadership. It refers to the internal dialogue that individuals initiate with themselves, which determines their behavior. Positive self-talk is believed to build an individual's self-confidence.

Advantages of Self-leadership

Digital entrepreneurs and other business-minded individuals can become their best leaders by fully embracing the process of self-leadership. They can achieve more than they ever thought possible by setting personal goals, maintaining motivation, and managing time and resources effectively. Self-leadership is about taking responsibility for one's own success and happiness, knowing what you want, and pursuing it despite any obstacles that may arise.

As a self-leader, you don't wait for bosses or others to tell you what to do or give you permission or validation to succeed. You are on your way to translating your dreams into reality, taking control of your life, charting your own course, making your own decisions, and doing whatever it takes to reach your strategic goals. Research findings suggest that there are numerous additional benefits to practicing self-leadership, which include[56]:

- Increased task commitment and responsibility due to enhanced self-leadership skills.

- Better emotional control and decision-making abilities as a result

[56] See, for example, The Importance of Cultivating Self-leadership (www.selfleadership.com); The Ultimate Guide to Self-Leadership (https://fellow.app); Carmeli, Abraham et al (2006). Self-leadership Skills and Innovative Behavior at Work, *International Journal of Manpower*, 27(1), 75; Ghosh, Koustab (2015). Developing Organizational Crea-tivity and Innovation: Toward a Model of Self-leadership, Employee Creativity, Creativity Climate and Workplace Innovative Orientation, *Management Research Review*, 38(11), 1126-1148.

of self-leadership.

- Greater motivation, a clear vision, and a strategic outlook for individuals who practice self-leadership.

- Effective teamwork is more likely when individuals possess self-leadership qualities.

- The attributes of patience and task competency are commonly found in self-leaders.

- Improved productivity and efficiency are associated with individuals who exhibit self-leadership traits.

- Self-leadership encourages actions that align with ethical values.

- Self-leaders are a valuable human asset to any organization.

Self-leadership Skills

In order to become a self-leader, it is necessary for individuals to acquire the knowledge and skills required to master the essential ingredients of the self-leadership process, as indicated below:

- Awareness: being able to identify your own thoughts, strengths, weaknesses, values, and intentions in different situations.

- Accountability: taking responsibility for your actions and the choices you make.

- Self-control: managing your emotions and behavior effectively.

- Self-focus: being able to complete tasks in a timely manner.

- Social skills: networking via social media and other venues, building business relationships, and exhibiting a team player spirit.

- Persuasion: influencing friends, clients, and others to achieve desired goals.

- Goal-setting: creating goals and having the motivation and desire to accomplish them within a specified time frame.

- Decision-making: assessing alternative courses of action and selecting the best available option(s).

- Self-efficacy: the strong belief in one's own abilities, coupled with the confidence to effectively influence external factors, and ultimately achieve success in particular situations.

Now, you may ask, what are some practical steps individuals can take to develop their own self-leadership skills? Experts suggest the following[57]:

- Establish clear goals and track progress towards achieving them.

- Create a plan of action and monitor your progress.

- Overcome distractions and manage your time effectively.

- Seek help when you need it.

- Maintain a positive outlook towards oneself and the environment.

- Be proactive and resilient when communicating and interacting with others.

- Keep an open mind to new perspectives and ideas.

- Seek feedback from others to gain insight and improve performance.

- Ask thoughtful questions to enhance understanding and learning.

- Engage in regular reflection to evaluate progress and identify areas for growth.

- Explore your mindset to assess personal beliefs and attitudes.

- Reward yourself for your accomplishments.

Gaining self-leadership competencies can benefit individuals in several ways, including enhancing their self-confidence and creativity, improving their social relationships, increasing their situational adaptability, and

---

[57] See, for example, Developing Self-Leadership Competencies, Pen State Extension, https://etemsion.psu.edu; Posi-tive Psychology.com, Developing Self-leadership, Your Ultimate Coaching Guide, https://positiveosychology.com.

facilitating better decision-making and time management.

Emotional Intelligence

Emotional intelligence, as defined by the Oxford Languages dictionary, refers to the ability to recognize, regulate, and express one's emotions effectively, as well as to handle social interactions with sensitivity and discernment. This skill set is particularly critical for individuals striving for success, including entrepreneurs, and is intimately connected with self-leadership. Emotional intelligence and self-leadership are mutually interdependent, meaning they influence each other.

Daniel Goleman and Richard E. Boyatzis published an influential article in the Harvard Business Review on February 6, 2017, titled "Emotional Intelligence Has 12 Elements. Which Do You Need to Work On?" In the article, the authors identified four broad domains of emotional intelli-gence that include specific sub-elements:

1. Self-awareness, which refers to emotional self-awareness

2. Self-management, which includes emotional self-control, adaptability, achievement orientation, and positive outlook

3. Social awareness, which includes empathy and organizational awareness

4. Relationship management, which includes influence, coaching and mentoring, conflict management, teamwork, and inspirational leadership.

Studies have uncovered that within organizations, team leaders who possess high emotional intelligence positively impact the development of emotional intelligence at the group level. Furthermore, individuals who possess emotional intelligence skills tend to perform better and have higher prospects for career advancement within the organization. Additionally, salespeople who demonstrate emotional intelligence competencies are more likely to boost sales and enhance the quality of customer relationships for their firms. Emotional and social intelligence skills are critical factors in effective leadership, and individuals with well-developed emotional intelligence are better equipped to understand their own and others' feelings in social interactions.[58]

Time Management

Individuals who recognize the significance and worth of time, particularly those who bear numerous obligations like entrepreneurs, executives, and business owners, must acquaint themselves with techniques to amplify their productivity and efficiency. The practice of time management is a crucial skill to master, as it can improve an individual's ability to manage their time effectively within their organization and beyond.

Time management refers to the coordination of one's tasks, activities, meetings, and other professional responsibilities with the objective of maximizing their effectiveness, thereby enabling them to accomplish more and higher quality work in less time[59]. Authors have suggested numerous techniques to help individuals maximize their productivity while minimizing their effort, including:

- Get organized by using a daily planner and setting reminders for upcoming tasks.

- Prioritize and tackle the most challenging or difficult tasks when you feel most alert.

- Avoid or eliminate distractions, and resist the temptation to multitask.

- Set time limits for each task.

- Avoid procrastination; you have a maximum of 1,440 minutes per day.

- Identify where you are wasting your time.

- Delegate tasks to capable team members if possible.

---

[58] See, for example, Koman, Elizabeth S. and Wolff, Steven B. (2008). Emotional Intelligence Competencies in the Team and Team Leader: A Multi-level Examination of the Impact of Emotional Intelligence on team Performance, *Journal of Management Development,* 27(1), 55-77; Kunnanatt, James T. (2008). Emotional Intelligence: Theory and Description: A Competency Model for Interpersonal Effectiveness, Career Development *International,* 13(7), 614-629.

[59] Time Management, TechTarget Network, www.techtarget.com.

- Consider outsourcing some of the organization's functions.

Self-leadership and Innovation

An increasing amount of evidence indicates that individuals with self-leadership skills demonstrate a stronger inclination toward innovation. As we have previously discussed, self-leadership involves the capacity to take control of one's own behavior, thoughts, emotions, and actions to achieve desired results. It also encompasses goal-setting and motivation. On the other hand, innovation encompasses the introduction of new ideas, processes, and products or services that bring value to both consumers and organizations.

Self-leadership serves as a catalyst for innovation since it empowers individuals to actively and proactively explore novel approaches, methodologies, and ideas. It is probable that individuals possessing self-leadership attributes, such as self-motivation and self-control, are more likely to generate imaginative ideas and develop innovative products while also capitalizing on economic opportunities.

Similarly, the connection between self-leadership and invention is strong and enduring. Self-leadership significantly increases the likelihood of inventors achieving success with their ideas and projects. Inventors are often characterized by their creativity, persistence, and motivation. They adopt a strategic approach to their work and actively engage in problem-solving. Self-leadership skills are critical in supporting inventors as they strive to accomplish their goals and fulfill their aspirations.

It is worth noting that various factors, some of which are illustrated in the table below, can influence an individual's capacity for invention and innovation.

Table 1

Selected Ingredients of Invention and Innovation

Embrace curiosity	Explore fearlessly	Connect and cooperate with others
Cultivate and nourish your ideas	Embrace a variety of perspectives	Adopt a strategic mindset
Remain adaptable to change	Take charge and demonstrate self-leadership	Embrace the possibility of failure
Push yourself with challenging endeavors	Embrace change willingly	Embrace the power of creativity
Always think big	Show bravery in your actions	Dedicate time for innovation
Focus on taking action	Seek opportunities and stay focused on them	Hone and enhance your skills

See, for example, 12 characteristics of innovative people, https;//dobetteresade.edu; the 10 traits of great innovators, https://www.forbes.com; 11 proven habits of highly innovative people, https://www.entrepreneur.com.

Summary

Self-leadership is a vital aspect of an individual's personality that involves introspection, identifying strengths and weaknesses, exercising self-regulation, and managing relationships. It is an essential competence for digital and other entrepreneurs to possess, develop, and utilize to steer their teams and business endeavors toward sustainable growth and competitive advantage. The process of self-leadership involves individuals taking charge of their behavior, emotions, and actions. Key sources of self-leadership include self-awareness, self-motivation, self-discipline, and self-confidence.

The advantages of self-leadership are numerous, including better emotional regulation and decision-making abilities, increased motivation, clear strategic vision, and effective teamwork. Some of the essential skills required for self-leadership are self-control, self-focus, and social skills. Adopting an open-minded attitude towards novel ideas and perspectives and soliciting feedback from others to enhance performance are critical approaches for developing self-leadership skills. Experts also emphasize the importance of creativity, embracing change, and acknowledging the possibility of failure as crucial ingredients for invention and innovation.

Questions

1. Explore the fundamental nature of self-leadership and its significance for entrepreneurs.

2. Explain the essential skills necessary for individuals to be effective self-leaders.

3. Discuss the concept of emotional intelligence and its pertinence to the realm of digital marketing.

4. What are the essential qualities and actions one must possess to become an innovator? Provide a comprehensive explanation

References

Alsaaty, Falih M. (2023). Entrepreneurial Edge: Essentials for Business Success, Author Reputation Press, Company.

Bayo-Moriones, Alberto et al (2021). Business Strategy, Performance Appraisal and Organizational Results, *Personnel Review,* 50(2), 515-534.

Braa, Jorn et la. (2023). Design Theory for Societal Digital Transformation: The Case of Digital Global Health, *Journal of the Association for Information Systems,* 24(6), 1645-1669.

Cavallo, Angelo et al (2021). Competitive Intelligence and Strategy Formulation: Connecting the Dots, *Competitiveness Review,* 31(2), 250-275.

Certo, Samuel C. and Certo, S. Travis (2014). *Modern Management,* Boston: Massachusetts, Pearson Education, Inc.

David, Fred R. and David, Forest R. (2017). *Strategic Management,* Boston: Massachusetts, Pearson Education, Inc.

de Kluyver, Cornelis A. and Pearce II, John A. (2009). *Strategy – A View from the Top,* Upper Saddle: New Jersey, Pearson/Prentice-Hall, Inc.

Hill, Charles W. L., and Jones, Gareth R. (2013). *Strategic Management – Theory,* Mason: Ohio, Southwestern, Cengage Learning, Inc.

Mishra, Subrat P. and Mohanty, Brajarai (2022). Approaches to Strategy Formulations: A Content Analysis of Definitions of Strategy, *Journal of Management and Organization,* 28(6), 1133-1160.

Primorac, Dinko et al (2018). Entrepreneurial Orientation and Business Strategy – Analysis of Entrepreneurial Options: Evidence from Serbia, *Journal of Economic & Management Perspective,* 12(2), 589-595.

Rothaermel, Frank T (2015). *Strategic Management,* New York: NY, McGraw-Hill Education, Inc.

Senadjki, Abdelhak et al. (2024). Unlocking the potential: the impact of digital leadership On firms' performance through digital transformation, *Journal of Business and Socio-economic Development,* 4(2), 161-177.

Steiber, Annika et al. (2021). Digital transformation of industrial firms: An Innovation Diffusion Perspective, *European Journal of Innovative Management,* 24(3), 799-819.

Thompson, Arthur et at (2020). *Crafting and Executing Strategy,* New York: NY, McGraw-Hill Publications, Inc.

Weil, Nancy (March 1, 2009). CIO, 22(9).

Yang, Yunpeng et al (2023). The Digital Platform, Enterprise Digital Transformation, and Enterprise Performance of Cross-Border E-Commerce—From the Perspective of Digital Transformation and Data Elements, *Journal of Theoretical and Applied Electronic Com-merce Research,* 18(2), 777.

www.ingramcontent.com/pod-product-compliance
Lightning Source LLC
Chambersburg PA
CBHW052116030426
42335CB00025B/3003